JOSÉ ROBERTO A. IGREJA

Talking Business

 INGLÊS CORPORATIVO: REUNIÕES, APRESENTAÇÕES, NETWORKING, CONFERENCE CALLS E MUITO MAIS.

MAIS DE 400 EXPRESSÕES IDIOMÁTICAS DO MUNDO DOS NEGÓCIOS

CD de áudio para melhorar a compreensão e ativar a fluência

© 2018 José Roberto A. Igreja

Preparação de texto: **Elza Mendes**
Capa e projeto gráfico: **Paula Astiz**
Editoração eletrônica: **Paula Astiz Design**
Assistente editorial: **Mariana Lucas**

CD
Produtora: **jm produção de áudio**
Locutores: **Sarah Johnson, Melissa Trest Soares, Rodney Cameron, Michael Miller**

Dados Internacionais de Catalogação na Publicação (CIP)
(Câmara Brasileira do Livro, SP, Brasil)

Igreja, José Roberto A.
    Talking business / José Roberto A. Igreja. — 1. ed. — Barueri, SP : DISAL, 2018.

    ISBN 978-85-7844-195-1

    1. Conversação 2. Inglês — Atividades, exercícios etc. 3. Inglês comercial — Estudo e ensino 4. Negócios I. Título.

18-14061   CDD-428.3

Índices para catálogo sistemático:
1. Conversação comercial : Inglês : Linguística   428.3
2. Inglês : Conversação comercial : Linguística   428.3

Todos os direitos reservados em nome de:
Bantim, Canato e Guazzelli Editora Ltda.

Alameda Mamoré 911 – cj. 107
Alphaville – BARUERI – SP
CEP: 06454-040
Tel./Fax (11) 4195-2811
Visite nosso site: www.disaleditora.com.br
Televendas: (11) 3226-3111
Fax gratuito: 0800 7707 105/106
E-mail para pedidos: comercialdisal@disal.com.br

Nenhuma parte desta publicação pode ser reproduzida, arquivada ou transmitida de nenhuma forma ou meio sem permissão expressa e por escrito da Editora.

Apresentação 7

1 11
A HECTIC SCHEDULE
WORKING OVERTIME TO MEET DEADLINES

2 16
CORPORATE RELATIONSHIPS
A CONFLICT WITH THE NEW REGIONAL MANAGER

3 21
BUSINESS AS USUAL
PUTTING OUT FIRES AT WORK!

4 27
A NEW SUPPLIER
I GOOGLED THEM AND GUESS WHAT I FOUND OUT?

5 33
THE BOARD MEETING
HAVE YOU BEEN EAVESDROPPING ON THEM?

6 38
TECHNOLOGY
HEADING TOWARDS ANOTHER BIG REVOLUTION YET!

7 43
INNOVATION
THINKING OUT OF THE BOX

8
THE NEW GADGET
A PARADIGM SHIFT!

49

9
HIRING THE RIGHT PEOPLE
HAVE YOU MET THE NEW RECRUITS YET?

54

10
TRADE SHOWS
IS EVERYTHING ALL SET FOR THE HOUSTON FAIR?

59

11
ONLINE ADVERTISING
THEY SEEM TO BE INTERESTED IN OUR ONLINE CAMPAIGNS

65

12
A SHORT-STAFFED DEPARTMENT
THE WORKLOAD HAS BEEN INCREASING

70

13
A DREAM JOB
WHAT IS IT LIKE?

75

14
OPENING A NEW BRANCH
LET'S TAKE ONE STEP AT A TIME

80

15
BUSINESS GROWTH
THE SKY'S THE LIMIT!
86

16
MANUFACTURING
PLANNING AHEAD IS ESSENTIAL
92

17
MAKING PRESENTATIONS
I WAS WONDERING IF YOU COULD GIVE ME A FEW USEFUL TIPS
97

18
BUSINESS LUNCHES
I HATE TO TALK SHOP OVER MEALS!
103

19
THE MERGER DEAL
SCENARIOS
108

20
CORPORATE SCANDAL
HOW COULD A RESPECTFUL AND CLEVER EXECUTIVE GET INTO THIS?
114

Answer key
119

Glossary
149

Apresentação

Talking Business é um livro dirigido a todos que desejam melhorar o seu conhecimento de *Business English*, o inglês corporativo empregado no mundo dos negócios dos países de língua inglesa.

Com este livro você terá a oportunidade de aprender, revisar e consolidar inúmeras expressões e frases usuais empregadas em inglês por executivos de diversos segmentos profissionais. Você poderá também melhorar a escrita e a capacidade de se expressar em inglês comercial, bem como a compreensão auditiva através do áudio CD gravado por falantes americanos que acompanha o livro.

Veja abaixo as seções presentes no livro:

BUSINESS DIALOGUE

Talking Business apresenta 20 diálogos com temas atuais variados que versam sobre assuntos recorrentes do mundo dos negócios. Estes diálogos são repletos de expressões idiomáticas e outros termos usuais presentes no jargão do dia a dia das empresas em países de língua inglesa. As situações abordadas nos diálogos incluem:

- Trabalhando sobre pressão e alcançando as metas
- Lidando com conflitos nas empresas
- Tecnologia e inovação no mundo dos negócios
- Reuniões, apresentações e feiras comerciais
- Marketing online e mídias sociais
- Abrindo uma nova filial
- Relacionamento com fornecedores e funcionários da empresa
- Escândalo corporativo
- Fusões comerciais
- Planejamento e gerenciamento de um negócio
- Brainstorming, networking e conference calls

DIALOGUE COMPREHENSION – TRUE, FALSE OR I DON'T KNOW?

Oportunidade de conferir a compreensão das idéias apresentadas nos diálogos através da atividade *True, False or I don't know* contida nesta seção. Você poderá também checar as respostas desta atividade ao final do livro.

FOCUS ON WORDS & EXPRESSIONS

Esta seção explora as expressões e outros termos do mundo corporativo, que ganham vida nos contextos em que estão inseridos nos diálogos.

THE CORPORATE WORLD – USUAL PHRASES AND QUESTIONS

Você poderá conferir aqui uma seleção de perguntas e frases-chave recorrentes e características do mundo dos negócios. Uma boa maneira de absorver o conteúdo desta seção é ouvir o CD, que o ajudará a melhorar a compreensão auditiva relativa a variados temas importantes do dia a dia de uma empresa. Ao todo o livro apresenta 200 frases-chave presentes no discurso corporativo dos falantes de língua inglesa.

CORPORATE ACRONYMS & ABBREVIATIONS

Esta seção reúne siglas e abreviações muito usadas no mundo corporativo dos países de língua inglesa. Conhecer estes termos vai ajudar você a ter uma melhor compreensão de textos e diálogos comerciais.

BUSINESS VOCABULARY & EXPRESSIONS

Esta seção aborda novas palavras e expressões do mundo dos negócios através de uma atividade prática em que se deve combinar as definições apresentadas com os termos corporativos.

❋ GAP FILLING

São apresentadas 8 sentenças contextualizadas que devem ser completadas com o novo vocabulário e expressões abordadas na seção anterior. Um exercício interessante em que a diversidade das sentenças contextualizadas ajuda a consolidar o uso correto do vocabulário e expressões previamente apresentados.

❋ LISTEN & WRITE & ANSWER

Esta atividade objetiva desenvolver não somente a habilidade da compreensão auditiva, mas também da escrita, já que você deverá escrever 4 perguntas a partir da audição do CD. É também um exercício de múltipla escolha que trabalha o vocabulário e expressões apresentadas anteriormente.

Tenho certeza de que o conteúdo apresentado em todas as seções de ***Talking Business*** vai ajudar você a melhorar substancialmente o seu conhecimento de *Business English*, tornando-o mais confiante e apto à comunicação em inglês no âmbito corporativo e ajudando-o assim a avançar em sua carreira profissional.

ENJOY!

José Roberto A. Igreja

A HECTIC SCHEDULE
WORKING OVERTIME TO MEET DEADLINES

TRACK 1

Frank: What's your schedule like today?
Sheila: **Hectic!**
Frank: That makes two of us. I'll barely have time to **grab a bite** at the **cafeteria**.
Sheila: I know. I hate to work under pressure too. Seems like we've all been working **overtime** lately.
Frank: Gosh, I've been putting in so many extra hours so we can **meet the deadline** for our current project that I'm now beginning to feel stressed out.
Sheila: You're not the only one, but don't worry, help is on the way.
Frank: Help is on the way? What do you mean by that?
Sheila: I heard the company will be hiring some new people soon.
Frank: Seriously? You're not **pulling my leg**, are you?
Sheila: No, I'm serious. The **head honcho** is worried that some of us might suffer from **burnout**, you know.
Frank: Gee, Sheila, this is the best news I've heard in a long time.
Sheila: Sure! I feel the same. Anyway, it might take a while before the new **recruits** are ready to help us with the **workload**. Do you think you can **tough it out** a little longer?
Frank: I think so. I'm actually feeling much better after what you told me.
Sheila: Great, Frank. I have to go back to my **workstation** now. Talk to you later!
Frank: Sure, Sheila. It was nice talking to you! Bye!

DIALOGUE COMPREHENSION – TRUE, FALSE OR I DON'T KNOW?

1. Frank is not busy at all today.
   True ☐ False ☐ I don't know ☐
2. Sheila doesn't like working under pressure.
   True ☐ False ☐ I don't know ☐
3. Sheila has lunch at the company cafeteria every day.
   True ☐ False ☐ I don't know ☐
4. Frank and Sheila's boss is suffering from burnout.
   True ☐ False ☐ I don't know ☐

FOCUS ON WORDS & EXPRESSIONS

Find words or expressions in the dialogue that mean the same as:

a. The amount of work that a person has to do: _____

b. Extra hours that someone works in addition to their usual job hours: _____

c. The most important person in an organization; the top boss: _____

d. Marked by intense activity; very busy: _____
e. Finish something in time: _____
f. Physical or emotional exhaustion as a result of prolonged stress or overwork: _____

g. Telling me something that is not true as a joke: _____

h. Eat something: _____
i. A new member in a company or an organization, especially someone who has recently been hired: _____
j. A self-service restaurant, often in a factory or an office building where people select their food and drink at a counter and take it to a table to eat: _____
k. A desk with a computer in an office for someone to work at: _____

l. Go on with something in spite of difficulties; stand a situation: _____

A HECTIC SCHEDULE

THE CORPORATE WORLD – USUAL PHRASES AND QUESTIONS 1
TRACK 2

Our workload has practically doubled in the past few months.
What's your schedule like today?
I've got a pretty tight schedule today.
Sorry, I can't talk to you now. Can I call you back later?
The new manager is very demanding.
I haven't had a vacation in a long time.
How about a break?
I need to take some days off.
I badly need a vacation.
Let's call it a day!

CORPORATE ACRONYMS & ABBREVIATIONS 1

ROI = Return On Investment
TM = Trademark
CEO = Chief Executive Officer
NGO = Non-governmental Organization
ISO = International Standardization Organization

 BUSINESS VOCABULARY & EXPRESSIONS 1

Match the words and expressions below to the definitions:

1. RUN A BUSINESS	**5.** CORE BUSINESS
2. TWENTY-FOUR SEVEN	**6.** BEHIND SCHEDULE
3. ABSENTEEISM	**7.** BOSSY
4. CALL IT A DAY	**8.** SWAMPED (WITH WORK)

A. A company's main activity. ( )

WORKING OVERTIME TO MEET DEADLINES

B. Declare an end to the day's activities; end a day's work. ( )
C. Overburdened with work. ( )
D. The state of being absent from work. ( )
E. Manage a business; be in charge of a company. ( )
F. Running late. ( )
G. Tending to give orders to others; authoritarian. ( )
H. Twenty-four hours per day, seven days per week; all the time. ( )

GAP FILLING 1

Use the business vocabulary and expressions in the box to fill in the gaps in the sentences below:

CALL IT A DAY	SWAMPED (WITH WORK)	BOSSY
BEHIND SCHEDULE	TWENTY-FOUR SEVEN	ABSENTEEISM
	RUN A BUSINESS	CORE BUSINESS

1. Some convenience stores in big urban centers are open _____.
2. "As you know we are _____ with our current project. I think we'll have to put in some extra work over the next few days." said the general manager to his team.
3. "Our strategy has always been to focus on our _____ and outsource our non-core activities.", said George at the meeting.
4. I don't like working with the new regional manager because he's way too _____.
5. "Sorry, I can't talk to you right now. I'm _____ with work.", Dave told a friend over the phone.
6. "We've done enough work for today. Let's _____.", Bill told a coworker.
7. Mr. Drake Jr. has been _____ the family _____ since his father passed away.
8. What can employers do to reduce _____ rates in the workplace?

14 A HECTIC SCHEDULE

LISTEN & WRITE & ANSWER 1

🎧 TRACK 3

Write the questions you listen to and then choose the right answer:

1. _____?
- **a.** I do. I often go by car.
- **b.** About three times a week.
- **c.** About twenty minutes.
- **d.** I enjoy my subway commute because it gives me time to read the news online.

2. _____?
- **a.** I know, I hate deadlines too.
- **b.** September, 15th, but don't worry, we're ahead of schedule.
- **c.** Uh, I wouldn't talk to him right now if I were you. He's in a bad mood.
- **d.** We haven't hit any snags so far, so things are running smoothly.

3. _____?
- **a.** The manager needs those reports on his desk ASAP.
- **b.** They're getting along fine.
- **c.** No, I haven't been introduced to the new manager yet.
- **d.** Oh yeah, they're all very friendly.

4. _____?
- **a.** It's in Houston.
- **b.** We have branch offices all over the country.
- **c.** It's a great place to set up shop.
- **d.** There are about fifteen sales reps working here.

CORPORATE RELATIONSHIPS
A CONFLICT WITH THE NEW REGIONAL MANAGER

TRACK 4

Gary: Hey, Bill, how's it going?
Bill: Not bad, I guess.
Gary: You don't sound very enthusiastic. **Is something the matter?**
Bill: Well, since you're asking me, I guess I'll just be **plain** with you.
Gary: Sure, **getting it off your chest** will do you good. So, what's **bugging** you?
Bill: The new regional manager. I still haven't gotten used to him **breathing down my neck** all the time, you know.
Gary: Really?
Bill: Yeah, he's such a **control freak**! Honestly, I think he's **micromanaging** way too much. I just wish he would use his time more **wisely** and let us work in peace.
Gary: I had no idea he was like that. Do the other people in your department feel the same?
Bill: Pretty much so.
Gary: You know, Bill, the company he used to work for has a different **corporate culture**, and he's been here for just a couple of weeks. Maybe he needs some more time to get used to the way we work here.
Bill: I guess!
Gary: I'll tell you what, I'll talk to our human resources director and see what we can do about this. I'm sure Michael can take care of it. He's a great conflict manager.
Bill: Gee, Gary, that would be great! Thanks a million!
Gary: You're welcome, Bill!

DIALOGUE COMPREHENSION – TRUE, FALSE OR I DON'T KNOW?

1. Bill is the only one in his department who's not happy about the new regional manager.
   True ☐   False ☐   I don't know ☐
2. Gary shows sympathy and is willing to help.
   True ☐   False ☐   I don't know ☐
3. Bill is planning to change jobs soon.
   True ☐   False ☐   I don't know ☐
4. According to Gary, the new regional manager needs to adapt to their corporate culture.
   True ☐   False ☐   I don't know ☐

FOCUS ON WORDS & EXPRESSIONS

Find words or expressions in the dialogue that mean the same as:

a. Closely observing and controlling in a detailed manner the work of one's employees: _____

b. Putting pressure on me: _____

c. Someone with an obsessive need to exert control over situations and people: _____

d. Annoying: _____

e. The values, behavior and dress code of a corporation: _____

f. Honest; open: _____

g. Telling someone about something that has been annoying you: _____

h. Is something wrong?; any problem?: _____

i. Prudently; showing good sense or good judgment: _____

THE CORPORATE WORLD – USUAL PHRASES AND QUESTIONS 2
TRACK 5

Do you get along with the new manager?
I can't stand the way Mike is always whining about everything
Why don't you tell me what's bothering you?
I hate the way my boss is always bossing me around!
He's always been a hardworking employee.
Is your new boss very demanding?
I don't like the new manager's bossy style.
What's the deadline for your current project?
Does the new marketing director have a good rapport with his staff?
What's the new boss like?

CORPORATE ACRONYMS & ABBREVIATIONS 2

KBI = Key Business Indicators
HQ = Headquarters
dept = department
ETA = Estimated Time of Arrival
CFO = Chief Financial Officer

 BUSINESS VOCABULARY & EXPRESSIONS 2

Match the words and expressions below to the definitions:

1. IN CHARGE OF	5. BOSS AROUND
2. DEMANDING	6. CALL THE SHOTS
3. PLAY HARDBALL	7. EAGER BEAVER
4. PEER	8 LAID-BACK

A. Give orders; make the decisions ( )
B. A person who is hardworking and enthusiastic. ( )

18   CORPORATE RELATIONSHIPS

C. Responsible for. ( )
D. Someone who belongs to the same professional group as another person. ( )
E. Calm and relaxed; easy-going; not worried about things that need to be done. ( )
F. Work or act aggressively, competitively or ruthlessly. ( )
G. Requiring a lot of attention, time or resources. ( )
H. Give orders, esp. in an unpleasant way; keep telling someone what to do. ( )

GAP FILLING 2

Use the business vocabulary and expressions in the box to fill in the gaps in the sentences below:

BOSS AROUND	LAID-BACK	DEMANDING	EAGER BEAVER
IN CHARGE OF	PLAY HARDBALL	PEER	CALL THE SHOTS

1. "I need to talk to the person _____ accounts payable please.", said Mr. Smith over the phone.
2. "Is your new boss very _____?", Carla asked a friend.
3. "The new manager has a very aggressive style. I don't think he will put up with _____ employees.", said Martha to a coworker.
4. Some people believe you have to _____ to move up the corporate ladder.
5. "If you want to talk business, you have to see Nicholas. He's the one who _____ around here.", said Dave to the newcomer.
6. "I wish you would stop _____ me _____.", said Jill to a coworker.
7. Ronald seems to have a good rapport with his _____.
8. The new sales rep gets to work early every morning. He's a real _____.

LISTEN & WRITE & ANSWER 2

 TRACK 6

Write the questions you listen to and then choose the right answer:

1. _____?
- **a.** Sure, they have to wear a uniform every day.
- **b.** No, I don't have to wear a suit and a tie to work.
- **c.** It's pretty casual and I like it that way.
- **d.** Yes, we do have casual Fridays.

2. _____?
- **a.** No, that won't bother me at all.
- **b.** Uh, OK, maybe I'd better get it off my chest.
- **c.** Sure, all the bugs have been ironed out.
- **d.** I agree. Doing that was a pain in the neck to say the least.

3. _____?
- **a.** Sorry, I haven't finished the report yet.
- **b.** I don't know who he reports to.
- **c.** Of course I did. I e-mailed it to you in the morning.
- **d.** I do. We get along fine.

4. _____?
- **a.** He's demanding, but he's also very considerate and supportive.
- **b.** Sure, I've already been introduced to him.
- **c.** I did. I met him last Tuesday.
- **d.** I don't think I agree with his managing style.

BUSINESS AS USUAL
PUTTING OUT FIRES AT WORK!

TRACK 7

Tony: Hey, Steve! How's it going? You look kind of tired.

Steve: I'm okay, but I'm feeling a little stressed out. I've had to **put out** more **fires** than usual at work recently.

Tony: I see. I've also had a **rough** week in the office. We have three coworkers **on leave** right now and our **workload** has increased considerably.

Steve: Yeah, I know exactly what you're talking about. My department is **short-staffed**. We need to **hire** at least two more qualified professionals **ASAP**. **Other than that** things are coming along fine, I mean business is **booming** and we've had record sales in the past two **quarters**.

Tony: Great! It's good to hear that. I can't complain either. My company seems to be growing really fast and they are treating us very well. What kind of **perks** do you guys get at your company?

Steve: Uh, it depends a lot on the position, but I'd say the benefits offered are quite generous. All managers get a company car, a notebook computer and a cell phone.

Tony: Sounds great! By the way, do you have **casual Friday**?

Steve: We do. I mean, the office people do, not the factory guys. They have to wear a uniform every day. I really enjoy dressing more informally on Fridays, we all feel more **at ease** and it does help create a more relaxed atmosphere in the office, you know.

Tony: Sure, I agree with you completely. I think casual Friday is great!

Steve: So your company is growing fast, right? I bet the **prospects** for promotion must be really good.

Tony: They are and I'm really excited about them. I'm really glad I get along with all my **peers** and fortunately I have a great relationship with my boss.

Steve: That's really important. My boss is very demanding, but he's also very supportive and kind. It's great to work with him. So, I remember you told me you're going on vacation soon, aren't you?

Tony: I am. Three weeks from now actually.

Steve: Great! Are you guys traveling anywhere for vacation?

Tony: Yep, we're visiting my wife's family up in Pittsburgh. Most of my in-laws live there, so we'll be there for a week.

Steve: Sounds like fun. I think it will also be a great time for you to **recharge your batteries**. Enjoy!

Tony: Thanks, Steve!

DIALOGUE COMPREHENSION – TRUE, FALSE OR I DON'T KNOW?

1. Tony's and Steve's companies are both doing well.
   True ☐   False ☐   I don't know ☐
2. Steve often goes jogging in parks to relax.
   True ☐   False ☐   I don't know ☐
3. Both Tony and Steve like casual Friday.
   True ☐   False ☐   I don't know ☐
4. Steve is going on vacation soon.
   True ☐   False ☐   I don't know ☐

FOCUS ON WORDS & EXPRESSIONS

Find words or expressions in the dialogue that mean the same as:

a. Rest for a period of time in order to feel energetic again: _____

b. Without enough workers: _____

c. Growing rapidly: _____
d. The amount of work that a person has to do: _____
e. As soon as possible: _____
f. Deal with urgent problems at work: _____
g. Employ: _____
h. Absent with permission from work or duty: _____
i. Difficult: _____
j. The possibility of future success: _____
k. A working day on which it is acceptable to dress casually at work: _____
l. Benefits beyond regular pay: _____
m. A period of three months: _____
n. Relaxed: _____
o. People who belong to the same professional group as another person: _____
p. Besides that: _____

THE CORPORATE WORLD – USUAL PHRASES AND QUESTIONS 3
TRACK 8

Do you have to wear a suit and a tie to work?
How long have you been working for this company?
Don't talk to the boss right now. He seems to be in a bad mood.
What do you like to do to relax?
Do you often have to put out fires at work?
The new strategy to boost sales is pretty interesting.
Do you know why they have called off the meeting?
Is the dress code formal at your company?
The dress code where I work is pretty casual.
My commute to work takes just about fifteen minutes.

CORPORATE ACRONYMS & ABBREVIATIONS 3

CV = Curriculum Vitae (résumé)
BTW = By the way
COD = Cash On Delivery
HR = Human Resources
N/A = Not Applicable

BUSINESS VOCABULARY & EXPRESSIONS 3

Match the words and expressions below to the definitions:

1. ON DUTY	5. ALL SET
2. GAME PLAN	6. RED TAPE
3. STAFF	7. HIGHLIGHTS
4. TEAMWORK	8. AT STAKE

A. The most significant or interesting parts of something. ( )
B. Too much paperwork that slows down business; bureaucracy. ( )
C. Cooperative effort done by a team in order to achieve a common goal. ( )
D. A group of people who work for a company. ( )
E. At risk; in danger of being lost. ( )
F. Ready. ( )
G. Doing one's job; at work. ( )
H. Plan of action; strategy. ( )

24   BUSINESS AS USUAL

GAP FILLING 3

Use the business vocabulary and expressions in the box to fill in the gaps in the sentences below:

| HIGHLIGHTS | TEAMWORK | RED TAPE | AT STAKE |
| STAFF | ALL SET | ON DUTY | GAME PLAN |

1. "You have to have a _____ for your career if you want to move up the corporate ladder.", said Sean to a friend.
2. "Jeff works for a small company with a _____ of just over twenty employees.", Hank told Monica.
3. "I'll be _____ from noon to nine pm today.", said Don to a friend.
4. "Can you brief me on the _____ of the conference?", Gary asked a coworker.
5. "Some of the applicants interviewed this week showed great _____ skills.", said the human resources manager to a coworker.
6. "I wish there was a way to cut through the _____ and speed up the process.", said Richard to a coworker.
7. "We'd better call a meeting ASAP and try to come up with a solution to this problem. There's a lot _____ here.", Mr. Gordon told his team.
8. "Is everything _____ for the presentation tomorrow morning?", Howard asked Melanie.

LISTEN & WRITE & ANSWER 3

TRACK 9

Write the questions you listen to and then choose the right answer:

1. _____?
   a. Yes, it's already been scheduled.
   b. The shareholders are not aware of what's been going on here.
   c. I don't have a clue.
   d. I have no idea what's on the agenda.

PUTTING OUT FIRES AT WORK! 25

2. _____?
- **a.** I have no doubt about it. The work environment does feel more relaxing when people are dressed casually.
- **b.** It's pretty casual. I often wear sneakers to work.
- **c.** He's in a bad mood now.
- **d.** Jim's always in a good mood. That's why everybody likes him.

3. _____?
- **a.** I don't think it will help us boost sales.
- **b.** We can probably do without it. Let's see how things pan out first.
- **c.** It provides high speed internet service.
- **d.** Sure, all important news and messages are posted on the intranet. It's very useful.

4. _____?
- **a.** I'm doing fine, thanks! How about you?
- **b.** Pretty good. We've reached all our sales goals for the past three quarters.
- **c.** No, I'm not doing that today. I'm busy with something else.
- **d.** I have no idea what they're doing now. Why don't you ask Carol?

A NEW SUPPLIER
I GOOGLED THEM AND GUESS WHAT I FOUND OUT?

TRACK 10

Howard: Hi, Damon, how's it going? I haven't seen you around much lately.
Damon: I've been pretty busy with the new project. That's why! By the way, do you think you could **e-mail** me the last version of the financial spreadsheet?
Howard: Sure, I'll do that first thing when I get back to the office.
Damon: Thanks!
Howard: Remember that company we talked about the other day?
Damon: You mean the office equipment company?
Howard: Yeah, I **googled** them and guess what I found out?
Damon: **I don't have a clue**. What did you find out?
Howard: They supply office equipment to many companies in this region, including some of our **competitors**.
Damon: Really? It might be a good idea to find out more about their services and prices.
Howard: Sure, I was thinking, maybe we should **set up a meeting** with one of their **sales reps**, what do you think?
Damon: Definitely. Let's do that. Sorry, I gotta run now. The **head honcho** wants the sales report on his desk **ASAP**. I've been working on it for two days now and I gotta **wrap it up**.
Howard: Sure, Damon, I was going to invite you out for lunch today. Do you think you can make it?
Damon: Not today, I'm **swamped with work** so I'll probably just **grab a bite** at the company **cafeteria**. I'll **take a rain check** though.
Howard: Sure, Damon, maybe some other time.

Damon: Thanks anyway. I'll see you around. Bye.
Howard: Bye.

❙ DIALOGUE COMPREHENSION – TRUE, FALSE OR I DON'T KNOW? ❙

1. Damon can't go out for lunch with Howard today.
   True ☐   False ☐   I don't know ☐
2. Howard doesn't like eating at the company cafeteria.
   True ☐   False ☐   I don't know ☐
3. Damon has been working on the sales report for about a week now.
   True ☐   False ☐   I don't know ☐
4. Both Howard and Damon think they should find out more about the office equipment supplier.
   True ☐   False ☐   I don't know ☐

❧ FOCUS ON WORDS & EXPRESSIONS ❧

Find words or expressions in the dialogue that mean the same as:

a. The top boss; the most important person in an organization: _____

b. Schedule a meeting: _____

c. I have no idea: _____

d. Send an e-mail or e-mails to someone: _____

e. Finish it: _____

f. A company that sells the same products or services as another company: _____

g. Sales representatives: _____

h. A computer program for financial calculations: _____

i. Eat something: _____

j. As soon as possible: _____

k. Search for information on the Web, normally using the Google search engine: _____

l. A self-service restaurant, often in a factory or an office building where people select their food and drink at a counter and take it to a table to eat: _____

m. Postpone until a later time: _____

n. Overburdened with work: _____

THE CORPORATE WORLD – USUAL PHRASES AND QUESTIONS 4
TRACK 11

What's your take on our competitor's new product line?
I have my hands full with this new project.
Have you ever worked on the night shift?
How many sales reps will the company hire?
Can we have a quick meeting to talk about those pending issues?
Do you keep track of your monthly expenses with stationery?
Have you told them about the new policy yet?
There's been a growing demand for this kind of product recently.
I'm sure we could boost sales with this new strategy.
Can you give me a ballpark figure on how much that would cost?

CORPORATE ACRONYMS & ABBREVIATIONS 4

MBA = Master of Business Administration
COO = Chief Operating Officer
AGM = Annual General Meeting
max = maximum
ISP = Internet Service Provider

❋ BUSINESS VOCABULARY & EXPRESSIONS 4

Match the words and expressions below to the definitions:

1. BAIL OUT	5. PLAN AHEAD
2. FACILITIES	6. WORKAHOLIC
3. DAY OFF	7. CALL A MEETING
4. ON TOP OF THINGS	8. PURCHASE

A. Make preparations or arrangements for the future. ( )
B. Buy. ( )
C. Someone with a compulsive need to work. ( )
D. Schedule a meeting. ( )
E. Equipment and services provided for a particular purpose. ( )
F. In control of what is happening. ( )
G. Help a company or someone out of a difficult situation, often by giving them money. ( )
H. A day when you're not required to work. ( )

❋ GAP FILLING 4

Use the business vocabulary and expressions in the box to fill in the gaps in the sentences below:

WORKAHOLIC	PURCHASE	CALL A MEETING	BAIL OUT
ON TOP OF THINGS	PLAN AHEAD	DAY OFF	FACILITIES

1. "Larry likes to be _____, so we'd better keep him posted.", said Brian at the meeting.
2. The company is headquartered in a high-tech office building offering all kinds of modern _____.
3. The marketing manager plans to _____ soon to talk about the new product line.
4. Mr. Dickson hardly ever goes on vacation. He's also the first one to arrive in the office and the last one to leave. He's a confirmed _____.

30   A NEW SUPPLIER

5. "Where can we _____ that kind of machine?", Jason asked Robin.
6. "They may have to close down the business if no one _____ them _____.", said Howard to his friends.
7. "I like to go jogging in the park and get a tan on my _____.", said Michael to a coworker.
8. When it comes to business it's always good to _____.

❋ LISTEN & WRITE & ANSWER 4

🎧 TRACK 12

Write the questions you listen to and then choose the right answer:

1. _____?
   a. I don't have a clue what his marital status is.
   b. I think so, but let me double check it.
   c. I heard she got engaged last month.
   d. Things are running smoothly. We'll surely meet the deadline, don't worry!

2. _____?
   a. We'd appreciate if you could give us some feedback.
   b. Sure, I'll keep in touch with you and let you know if anything else happens.
   c. The response has been very positive so far, but we still need to wait a little longer.
   d. Unfortunately we've hit some snags so I'm not sure we'll meet the deadline.

3. _____?
   a. Definitely. We have a great game plan and I'm sure it's going to work just fine.
   b. They have increased their market share by 20%.
   c. Those are the new market trends it seems.
   d. I'm sure we'll reach all our sales goals for the quarter.

4. _____?
   a. It should take some time before they release it.
   b. That will depend on what happens next.
   c. My commute to work takes just about ten minutes now that I've moved.
   d. I think that new toy is great. I've never seen anything like that, honestly, I think it will be a hit with the kids.

THE BOARD MEETING
HAVE YOU BEEN EAVESDROPPING ON THEM?

TRACK 13

Frankie: Hey, Josh! Great to see you.
Josh: Hi, Frankie, how's it going?
Frankie: Pretty good! Man, you have no idea what's about to happen at the company.
Josh: What's about to happen at the company? What do you mean? Have they posted any news on the company's **intranet** that I haven't seen yet?
Frankie: **Nope**, but I just happen to have some **first-hand** news.
Josh: First-hand news? What are you talking about?
Frankie: Well, this is coming right out of the board meeting. I will only tell you if you promise to keep it a secret.
Josh: You mean to say **you've attended** the board meeting?
Frankie: Not really, but you know, my **cubicle** is quite close to the meeting room and they left the door half open, so I couldn't help listening to what they were saying.
Josh: You've been **eavesdropping o**n them? Gosh, Frankie! This is really unacceptable!
Frankie: Hey, take it easy! I just happened to be at the right place at the right time, that's all!
Josh: At the right place at the right time? What is this? Some kind of a joke? I'm sorry, Frankie, I have no interest in listening to what you have to say.
Frankie: Aren't you curious?
Josh: No, not at all, so let's please just **drop the subject**, if you don't mind.

Frankie: Ok, Josh. I guess sooner or later everyone will find out anyway, I just thought you might like to know about it **beforehand**.

Josh: Thanks, Frankie, but no thanks! Ok. I gotta run back to my office, I have a couple of reports that I need to **wrap up**.

Frankie: Sure, Josh. I guess I'll see you around then. Take care!

DIALOGUE COMPREHENSION – TRUE, FALSE OR I DON'T KNOW?

1. Frankie has been invited to attend the board meeting.
   True ☐   False ☐   I don't know ☐
2. Josh thinks Frankie shouldn't have done what he did.
   True ☐   False ☐   I don't know ☐
3. Josh promised to keep it a secret.
   True ☐   False ☐   I don't know ☐
4. Frankie will surely be fired for what he did.
   True ☐   False ☐   I don't know ☐

FOCUS ON WORDS & EXPRESSIONS

Find words or expressions in the dialogue that mean the same as:

a. In advance: _____
b. A private computer network that can be accessed only by the employees of a company: _____
c. No: _____
d. Listening secretly: _____
e. You have been present at: _____
f. A work area that is partly separated from the rest of a room in an office: _____
g. Stop talking about it: _____
h. Finish something completely: _____
i. Coming directly from the original source: _____

THE CORPORATE WORLD – USUAL PHRASES AND QUESTIONS 5
TRACK 14

Have you attended the board meeting?
Where will the conference be held?
Things are looking up for the next quarter!
How long will the meeting last?
Will your company have a booth at the upcoming tech show in Vegas?
We're running low on A4 paper and staples.
Has the printer been fixed yet?
The copy machine is jammed. Do you know how to fix it?
They expect to do the launch of their new product next month.
Thank you all for attending this meeting!

CORPORATE ACRONYMS & ABBREVIATIONS 5

CRM = Customer Relationship Management
PO = Post Office
TQM = Total Quality Management
wk. = week
CPU = Central Processing Uni

BUSINESS VOCABULARY & EXPRESSIONS 5

Match the words and expressions below to the definitions:

1. BALLPARK FIGURE
2. PLUMMET
3. BY THE BOOK
4. SET UP SHOP
5. TAKE A TOLL ON
6. CRUNCH NUMBERS
7. STATS
8. SHIFT

A. Calculate carefully; do the math. (   )
B. Fall quickly; decrease rapidly in value or amount. (   )

HAVE YOU BEEN EAVESDROPPING ON THEM?

C. Statistics. ( )
D. Rough estimate or figure. ( )
E. Start a business; create a place to do business. ( )
F. A period of work time. ( )
G. Show wear and tear on someone or something; to damage. ( )
H. According to the rules. ( )

GAP FILLING 5

Use the business vocabulary and expressions in the box to fill in the gaps in the sentences below:

| STATS | SHIFT | TAKE A TOLL ON | BALLPARK FIGURE |
| BY THE BOOK | SET UP SHOP | PLUMMET | CRUNCH NUMBERS |

1. "I heard they _____ back in the early 70's, with a small office in New Jersey.", said Luke to a friend.
2. The accountants have been _____ all day trying to figure out if it's worth replacing the old machines for new ones.
3. According to the _____ demand for this kind of product has been increasing.
4. Working eleven hours a day is starting to _____ Ronald.
5. "Can you give me a _____ on how much you're planning to spend?", Jake asked Ronald.
6. "How many people work on the night _____?", Harry asked the plant manager.
7. "Seems like stock prices have _____ again today.", Fred told a friend.
8. "I was really surprised when I heard about that company's shady deals since they had always done everything _____.", said Barry to a coworker.

LISTEN & WRITE & ANSWER 5

TRACK 15

Write the questions you listen to and then choose the right answer:

1. _____?
- **a.** They've invested in stocks.
- **b.** As much as necessary, I do believe this is crucial to us.
- **c.** He's not willing to cooperate.
- **d.** I agree, investing in the stock market can be a risky business.

2. _____?
- **a.** We may need to implement a new shift if demand for our products keeps up.
- **b.** Sure, why not? Brainstorming has always been an efficient way to come up with interesting ideas.
- **c.** I think so. He's used to it.
- **d.** No, I could never do that. I don't think it's healthy.

3. _____?
- **a.** No, but we may need to hire a new one soon.
- **b.** Sure, I think he's our best sales rep.
- **c.** I think he might be promoted.
- **d.** Yeah, definitely. That's what it looks like.

4. _____?
- **a.** Sure, it's brand-new equipment.
- **b.** It's too early to tell, let's take one step at a time.
- **c.** Uh, I think five thousand dollars is a good ballpark figure.
- **d.** Let's call a meeting to talk about next month's budget.

6

TECHNOLOGY
HEADING TOWARDS ANOTHER BIG REVOLUTION!

🎧 TRACK 16

Jake: Man, it's amazing how technology is changing the way we do business. These are really exciting times!

Howard: **You can say that again**. I find it hard to keep up with all the new **gadgets** and **apps** that are popping up all the time now.

Jake: I know! You just reminded me of the taxi driver I talked to the other day. I was really surprised when he told me most of his passengers now contact him through an app. From what he told me it seems to be a very **ingenious** and helpful one.

Howard: Yeah, there are apps for just about anything now. They are making people's lives easier in many ways. Now, something else that's really cool is **3D printing**.

Jake: I agree. I think the impact of 3D printing on our daily lives will be massive. Can you imagine being able to print objects in the comfort of your home?

Howard: Yeah, it's crazy! 3D printing is **bound to** change many industries as we know them. Take the automobile industry for example. Medicine will also benefit greatly from 3D printing. I read an article about it the other day. Researchers are already using three-dimensional printing to create models of the human heart so that doctors can use them to better help patients before an operation.

Jake: Wow, seems like we're **heading towards** another big revolution!

Howard: We are in fact heading towards another technological stage. They're calling it the Internet of Things.

Jake: The Internet of Things?
Howard: Yep, it's a new concept that basically describes the trend that all devices, services and appliances will someday be interconnected.
Jake: Really? Sounds like a **sci-fi** movie.
Howard: I know, but I guess it will be real **someday**!

DIALOGUE COMPREHENSION – TRUE, FALSE OR I DON'T KNOW?

1. Both Jake and Howard are excited about the impact of technology in the workplace.
   True ☐ False ☐ I don't know ☐
2. According to the dialogue 3D printing will probably not affect businesses and medicine that much.
   True ☐ False ☐ I don't know ☐
3. Howard thinks technology is making people's lives harder.
   True ☐ False ☐ I don't know ☐
4. Jake goes to work by taxi every day.
   True ☐ False ☐ I don't know ☐

FOCUS ON WORDS & EXPRESSIONS

Find words or expressions in the dialogue that mean the same as:

a. Small electronic devices or appliances: _____
b. Huge; very large in amount or degree: _____
c. Science fiction: _____
d. At some future time: _____
e. An application (computer program) especially one designed for a mobile device. _____
f. You are right; that's true (to agree with a statement): _____
g. The process of making a physical object from a three-dimensional digital model: _____
h. Very clever; innovative: _____
i. Certain or destined to: _____
j. Moving toward: _____

THE CORPORATE WORLD – USUAL PHRASES AND QUESTIONS 6
TRACK 17

I need to contact the webmaster of that website.
Would you like a printout of the document?
That gadget company is located in Silicon Valley.
Do we need a password to log onto the system?
You can check out their website for a list of upcoming events.
How many hours a day do you spend surfing the Web?
We can make a killing selling these high-tech gadgets.
Do you often buy things online?
It feels great to work for a cutting-edge company like ours.
Do you think drones will be used commercially some day?

CORPORATE ACRONYMS & ABBREVIATIONS 6

Wi-Fi = Wireless Fidelity
CAD = Computer-Aided Design
IP = Internet Protocol
CTO = Chief Technology Officer
www = world wide web

BUSINESS VOCABULARY & EXPRESSIONS 6

Match the words and expressions below to the definitions:

1. TREND
2. SILICON VALLEY
3. GEEK
4. CUTTING-EDGE
5. FLASH DRIVE
6. START-UP
7. HACKER
8. TABLET

A. A small device used to store digital data. (   )
B. Extremely modern and advanced. (   )

40 TECHNOLOGY

C. A computer programmer who uses his skills to gain illegal access to a computer network in order to steal, change or destroy information: ( )
D. Prevailing tendency. ( )
E. A type of lightweight portable computer. ( )
F. A new business that has just been started. ( )
G. A region in California well-known for its concentration of high-tech industries. ( )
H. An expert in a technical field, esp. computers. ( )

GAP FILLING 6

Use the business vocabulary and expressions in the box to fill in the gaps in the sentences below:

GEEK	FLASH DRIVE	TABLET	SILICON VALLEY
HACKER	TREND	CUTTING-EDGE	START-UP

1. "I'm sure our visitors will love our high-tech plant and the _____ _____ technology of our machines.", said Brian to a coworker.
2. "When it comes to business, keeping updated on the latest market _____ is crucial.", Walter told Jim.
3. "We've been invited to visit a high-tech company in _____ next week. I'm really excited about it.", said Josh to a friend.
4. "How long do you think it will take that _____ to break even?", Frank asked Elizabeth.
5. "Hey, Charlie, do you know any _____ who might be able to help me out with this new computer system?", Jeff asked Roy.
6. "We'd better back up all these files. Can you pass me that _____ _____ please?", Roger asked a coworker.
7. "This new _____ is likely to do well in the gadget market.", said Hank to a coworker.
8. "Apparently a _____ broke into the company's computer system and altered some of the information. They're still trying to figure out what happened.", Rachel told a friend.

HEADING TOWARDS ANOTHER BIG REVOLUTION!

LISTEN & WRITE & ANSWER 6

TRACK 18

Write the questions you listen to and then choose the right answer:

1. _____?
- **a.** That's right. You can get high-speed internet here.
- **b.** There must be one. Let's check again.
- **c.** It's greatbreakcafe 123.
- **d.** I think we might be able to break the code.

2. _____?
- **a.** I don't think that would really be necessary.
- **b.** Uh, sorry! I may have done that by mistake.
- **c.** That's the storage capacity I guess.
- **d.** Just cross that name out and it will be okay.

3. _____?
- **a.** Not really. The digital version will do.
- **b.** I'd appreciate if you could e-mail that spreadsheet to me later.
- **c.** Sorry, I'm running out of ink.
- **d.** I think you forgot to attach the document.

4. _____?
- **a.** It seems like it's the new trend.
- **b.** I think it's time for an upgrade.
- **c.** I really need to catch up on my reading.
- **d.** I'm sure it will. I think it will be a hit with the young crowd.

INNOVATION
THINKING OUT OF THE BOX

🔘 TRACK 19

Ryan: How was the **brainstorming** session?
Dave: Interesting. I didn't expect we would **come up with** so many innovative ideas.
Ryan: Sounds good! So you plan on doing this again?
Dave: Definitely! We **gotta** hear what our people have to say. We have a **bright** team here and they can certainly contribute with their views and suggestions. I'll e-mail everyone with the **highlights** of the session later.
Ryan: Great! I'm curious. So, I heard Michael got transferred to our **branch office** in Baltimore.
Dave: That's right! He was having trouble **fitting in** with the sales team here. I'm sure he'll be doing okay there.
Ryan: I agree. What do you **make of** the new marketing director?
Dave: Well, I haven't talked to him much, but he seems to be **bold** and creative. He said he'll **call a meeting** soon so we can exchange some ideas about how to market our new **product line**.
Ryan: That's good news. I**'m looking forward to it**. You know, I think the problem with our previous director is that he never **thought out of the box** at all. He always had this **narrow-minded** view of everything.
Dave: I guess you're right. Innovation **plays a key role** in our industry, and real progress can only be made when you leave your comfort zone!

DIALOGUE COMPREHENSION – TRUE, FALSE OR I DON'T KNOW?

1. Dave plans to run some more brainstorming sessions in the future.
   True ☐   False ☐   I don't know ☐
2. Ryan's and Dave's company has branch offices all over the U.S.A.
   True ☐   False ☐   I don't know ☐
3. Michael got transferred to Baltimore because the company needed someone with his background there.
   True ☐   False ☐   I don't know ☐
4. Ryan thinks the previous marketing director was very creative and proactive.
   True ☐   False ☐   I don't know ☐

FOCUS ON WORDS & EXPRESSIONS

Find words or expressions in the dialogue that mean the same as:

a. The most significant or interesting parts of something: _____

b. Has a big influence on; is very important: _____

c. An office representing a company in a particular area: _____

d. A problem-solving technique in which members of a group spontaneously contribute ideas and suggestions: _____

e. Have to: _____
f. Intelligent: _____
g. Think freely, in an innovative way, using new ideas instead of traditional ones: _____
h. Think of a plan, idea, solution, etc.: _____

i. Schedule a meeting: _____

j. Courageous; brave; fearless and daring: _____
k. Be accepted by a group o people: _____

INNOVATION

l. A group of products marketed by a company: _____

m. Think of: _____

n. Not willing to accept new ideas, opinions or behavior that are different from your own: _____

o. I'm expecting it with pleasure; I'm excited about it: _____

THE CORPORATE WORLD – USUAL PHRASES AND QUESTIONS 7
TRACK 20

How's your new project coming along?
That was really thought-provoking, congrats!
I got a kick out of the presentation this morning.
He has always been very creative, no wonder he's in advertising!
The upcoming fair in Boston will be a great opportunity to showcase our products.
A lot of bright ideas came up during our brainstorming session.
I heard things are looking up for the next quarter.
Ok, let's roll up our sleeves and get down to business now.
Our company is doing really well, we're all excited about the prospects.
Do you know who's running the next brainstorming session?

CORPORATE ACRONYMS & ABBREVIATIONS 7

FYI = For Your Information
GDP = Gross Domestic Product
Info = Information
EU = European Union
CPA = Certified Public Accountant

BUSINESS VOCABULARY & EXPRESSIONS 7

Match the words and expressions below to the definitions:

1. SO FAR SO GOOD	5. PRICY
2. TAKE TIME OFF	6. HOLDING COMPANY
3. SMALL TALK	7. SUCK YOU DRY
4. NETWORKING	8. OFFICE SUPPLIES

A. Expensive. ( )
B. The practice of meeting other people involved in the same kind of work to exchange information. ( )
C. Supplies used in offices, such as paper clips, staples and A4 paper. ( )
D. Drain all your money. ( )
E. A company that controls other companies through stock ownership. ( )
F. Everything is OK up to this point. ( )
G. Have free time from work; take a break or vacation. ( )
H. Light, informal conversation about things that are not important. ( )

GAP FILLING 7

Use the business vocabulary and expressions in the box to fill in the gaps in the sentences below:

OFFICE SUPPLIES	SUCK YOU DRY	PRICY	SO FAR SO GOOD
HOLDING COMPANY	NETWORKING	SMALL TALK	TAKE TIME OFF

1. "I really need to _____ and relax. I've been feeling stressed out lately.", said Hank to a coworker.
2. "The upcoming trade show in Vegas will be a good opportunity to do some _____.", said Dave to a coworker.
3. "We're running low on some _____. Can you buy some A4 paper and staples next time you go to the stationery store?", Gordon asked Nick.

46   INNOVATION

4. "I can't afford to go to _____ restaurants right now.", said Jeff to a friend.
5. "Do you enjoy making _____ with strangers at parties?", Phillip asked Norman.
6. "If I were you I'd go easy on the slot machines. They can _____ you know.", Charlie advised Greg.
7. "A _____ doesn't really engage in any operations itself. It basically owns stocks of the companies it controls.", explained Donald at the meeting.
8. Barry: "So, Mike, how's your new job?".
   Mike: "_____ I've only been there for a week now, but I'm really enjoying it.".

LISTEN & WRITE & ANSWER 7

TRACK 21

Write the questions you listen to and then choose the right answer:

1. _____?
a. Sure, the game was really exciting.
b. I don't have a clue, but I think we'll find out soon enough. The marketing director has called a meeting to talk about it.
c. I wish I could go to the playoff game, but tickets are sold out.
d. I'm not sure who's in charge of that project.

2. _____?
a. Sounds like it's a great program!
b. I don't know. Maybe it's time to jump ship, you know what I mean, don't you?
c. I might do that. I'll let you know later.
d. They do. I actually met one of their interns a couple of weeks ago.

3. _____?
a. Sure, sir, hold on a second, I'll transfer your call.
b. I haven't met his secretary yet. What does she look like?
c. Sorry, I meant Mr. Harper, not Hopper!
d. I could certainly do that.

THINKING OUT OF THE BOX   47

4. _____?
   a. Sure, next Friday is fine. I'll see you then.
   b. Gee, I forgot to water the plants in my office this morning.
   c. No, unfortunately not. I think the factory guys would love to dress casually at least once a week, but they have to wear a uniform every day.
   d. I ran into him at the conference hall. I had no idea he'd be there.

THE NEW GADGET
A PARADIGM SHIFT!

🎧 TRACK 22

Roger: I have the feeling we're on to something big. This new digital watch combines some of the best **features** available today. I'm sure it will be **a hit** with the young crowd.

Brian: **You can say that again!** I'm really excited about the **prospects**. I'm sure this new **gadget** will **appeal** to a large number of people. Besides its **state-of-the-art** technology it's got a great design to it.

Roger: Sure! Do you think we'll have it ready to be launched at the next tech fair?

Brian: I'm not sure, I think it might take a while before we have a final version **up and running**. The next fair is coming up soon and **the clock is ticking** you know. I'd really rather not rush it, you know the saying, **haste makes waste**!

Roger: Right! I guess **you have a point** there, Brian. Ok, let's schedule a meeting with the tech team and find out what would be a **feasible timeline** for this new product. I can't wait to see it **hitting the shelves** of stores across the country. I think we'll be sending a new message to the market.

Brian: Really? What would that message be?

Roger: A **paradigm shift**!

Brian: Wow, Roger, I think **you nailed it**! That's right. A paradigm shift! It feels great to work for a company **at the cutting-edge** of digital technology like ours.

Roger: It sure does **pal**!

DIALOGUE COMPREHENSION – TRUE, FALSE OR I DON'T KNOW?

1. Brian is the CTO of the company.
   True ☐   False ☐   I don't know ☐
2. Roger doesn't sound very excited about their new product.
   True ☐   False ☐   I don't know ☐
3. Their new product is not quite ready yet.
   True ☐   False ☐   I don't know ☐
4. The company Roger and Brian work for is at the forefront of digital technology.
   True ☐   False ☐   I don't know ☐

FOCUS ON WORDS & EXPRESSIONS

Find words or expressions in the dialogue that mean the same as:

a. Viable; capable of being done: _____
b. At the most advanced stage of something: _____
c. Interest or attract someone: _____
d. Time is going by quickly: _____
e. A plan that shows when something should happen and how long it will take: _____
f. Important aspects of something: _____
g. The possibility of future success: _____
h. Actively working; functioning: _____
i. Small electronic device or appliance: _____
j. Something very successful: _____
k. You got it right!; that's exactly it: _____
l. Very modern; at the highest level of development: _____
m. You are right; that's true (to agree with a statement): _____
n. Hurrying can cause people to make mistakes: _____
o. Your idea is right: _____
p. Close friend; buddy: _____
q. Arrive in the stores; be available for sale: _____
r. The time when the usual way of doing something changes completely; a radical change in ideas or beliefs: _____

THE NEW GADGET

THE CORPORATE WORLD – USUAL PHRASES AND QUESTIONS 8
TRACK 23

When do you think the new system will be up and running?
Lots of new apps and gadgets are popping up all the time now.
Can you show me how to use this new app?
Do you think social media can help us get more customers?
What's your take on the new app that has just been released?
It seems that all their packaging is made of biodegradable material.
Their new product line looks great!
It takes more than just a good idea to launch a successful gadget.
We have to make sure we keep our products at affordable prices.
Do you think that new app will catch on?

CORPORATE ACRONYMS & ABBREVIATIONS 8

VoIP = Voice-over Internet Protocol
Yuppie = Young urban Professional
IT = Information Technology
e.g. = exempli gratia, for example
LCD = Liquid Crystal Display

BUSINESS VOCABULARY & EXPRESSIONS 8

Match the words and expressions below to the definitions:

1. TOUCH BASE WITH
2. BUDGET
3. AHEAD OF SCHEDULE
4. TRICKS OF THE TRADE
5. SPREADSHEET
6. OUT OF THE QUESTION
7. UPS AND DOWNS
8. IN THE PIPELINE

A. A computer program for financial calculations. ( )
B. Highs and lows; good and bad times. ( )

A PARADIGM SHIFT!   51

C. Being planned; in the process of being developed. ( )
D. Impossible. ( )
E. The amount of money a company has available to spend. ( )
F. Get in touch with; maintain contact. ( )
G. Special knowledge associated with a profession. ( )
H. Done earlier than the expected time. ( )

GAP FILLING 8

Use the business vocabulary and expressions in the box to fill in the gaps in the sentences below:

| UPS AND DOWNS | IN THE PIPELINE | BUDGET | OUT OF THE QUESTION |
| AHEAD OF SCHEDULE | TOUCH BASE WITH | SPREADSHEET |
| TRICKS OF THE TRADE |

1. "They've been in this business for such a long time that I'm sure they know all the _____."
2. "Can you e-mail the financial _____ to me later?", Kurt asked Jill.
3. The sales manager travels to San Francisco twice a month to _____ the sales people at the branch office there.
4. "That company you told me about is an active player in the market. Seems like they have lots of projects _____.", said Joe to a coworker.
5. "Buying a new machine now is _____. We simply can't afford it now.", said the financial manager at the meeting.
6. "This is a very competitive market so there will always be _____ in business, my friend.", said the manager to the new recruit.
7. "Apparently they run their business on a very tight _____.", said Bill to a friend.
8. "Fortunately we're _____ and will surely meet the deadlines for our current projects.", said Burt to a coworker.

LISTEN & WRITE & ANSWER 8

TRACK 24

Write the questions you listen to and then choose the right answer:

1. _____?
- **a.** No, I'm not familiar with it yet.
- **b.** That's right! It's a new app.
- **c.** Sure, I work every single day.
- **d.** Who knows? Let's wait and see what happens.

2. _____?
- **a.** I'm okay with that.
- **b.** I don't think they can afford it now.
- **c.** We do. We often use LinkedIn. It's designed specifically for the business community.
- **d.** I agree. Networking plays a major role in the corporate world.

3. _____?
- **a.** I usually do because that saves time, you know.
- **b.** I had a good first impression, but I need to learn more about them.
- **c.** They're planning the launch of their new product for the next quarter.
- **d.** Not that I know of.

4. _____?
- **a.** Sure, we set up a meeting for next week.
- **b.** That's what I needed to know, thanks!
- **c.** They seem to be excited about the upcoming trade show.
- **d.** Yep, everything's ready, don't worry!

A PARADIGM SHIFT!

HIRING THE RIGHT PEOPLE
HAVE YOU MET THE NEW RECRUITS YET?

TRACK 25

George: Hey, Vicky, you're an **early bird** today!
Vicky: Yep, I've been trying to leave home earlier so I can beat the **rush hour** traffic.
George: Yeah, I know. I often do the same. Have you met the new **recruits** yet?
Vicky: No, not yet. Have you?
George: Just two of them, Jake introduced them to me yesterday when I was **grabbing a bite to eat** at the **cafeteria**.
Vicky: Good! I'm looking forward to meeting them. So, what was your first impression?
George: Pretty good. They seem to be pretty smart and excited about their new job. I only talked to them briefly, but I can really tell you I got a pretty good impression of them.
Vicky: Sounds good! I actually **heard through the grapevine** that they're **a bunch of bright** kids. Do you know if Jake has already given them a tour of the company?
George: No, not yet, but he said he'll do it today.
Vicky: Perfect, I think I'll get a chance of meeting them today when they come to my department.
George: I'm sure you will, Vicky!

DIALOGUE COMPREHENSION – TRUE, FALSE OR I DON'T KNOW?

1. The new recruits haven't been given a tour of the company yet.
   True ☐   False ☐   I don't know ☐
2. George's commute to work takes about twenty minutes every day.
   True ☐   False ☐   I don't know ☐
3. Vicky has already met the new recruits.
   True ☐   False ☐   I don't know ☐
4. George often tries to beat the rush hour traffic.
   True ☐   False ☐   I don't know ☐

FOCUS ON WORDS & EXPRESSIONS

Find words or expressions in the dialogue that mean the same as:

a. A self-service restaurant, often in a factory or an office building where people select their food and drink at a counter and take it to a table to eat: _____

b. Hear news that has been passed from one person to another: _____

c. A new member in a company or an organization, especially someone who has recently been hired: _____

d. A group of: _____

e. Someone who wakes up and starts working very early; someone who gets somewhere or does something earlier than anyone else: _____

f. Intelligent: _____
g. Eating something: _____
h. Yes: _____
i. The time of day when traffic is heavy because many people are going to or coming from work: _____

THE CORPORATE WORLD – USUAL PHRASES AND QUESTIONS 9
TRACK 26

How long have you been working for that company?
He's always been a very hardworking employee.
I think he's too laid-back for this position.
How many people work in your department?
Monica is a multitasker. She can do a lot of things at the same time.
Jeff commutes to work by subway every day.
Do you get along well with your boss?
I have an excellent rapport with my peers.
Evelyn is very outgoing. She can mingle with the new people she meets easily.
Does your company have branch offices somewhere else?

CORPORATE ACRONYMS & ABBREVIATIONS 9

A.M. = Ante Meridiem, before noon
P.M. = Post Meridiem, after noon
pd. = paid
ATM = Automated Teller Machine
EPA = Environmental Protection Agency

 ## BUSINESS VOCABULARY & EXPRESSIONS 9

Match the words and expressions below to the definitions:

1. GUNG-HO
2. START FROM SCRATCH
3. BOTTOM LINE
4. IN A NUTSHELL
5. KINK
6. TEAM PLAYER
7. HIGHLIGHTS
8. COMPETITIVE EDGE

HIRING THE RIGHT PEOPLE

A. The most important thing to consider; the end result. ( )
B. Main corporate office. ( )
C. Clear advantage over the competition. ( )
D. Someone who works well with others. ( )
E. Using as few words as possible; very briefly. ( )
F. Small problem. ( )
G. Very enthusiastic. ( )
H. Start a project from the very beginning; start from nothing. ( )

GAP FILLING 9

Use the business vocabulary and expressions in the box to fill in the gaps in the sentences below:

| HEADQUARTERS | GUNG-HO | TEAM PLAYER | START FROM SCRATCH |
| COMPETITIVE EDGE | KINK | IN A NUTSHELL | BOTTOM LINE |

1. "I'm glad everyone seems to be _____ about our new project. Motivation is everything!", said the marketing director.
2. "We have a few _____ to work out with this project, but I'm sure it will be a very successful one.", Nick told a coworker.
3. "Sorry, I don't have time for long explanations now. Can someone give me the facts _____?
4. Knowing how to speak other languages can certainly give you a _____ when looking for a job.
5. "You mean they have built a solid company in just about two years and now hire 72 people? Can you believe they actually _____?", Donald asked a friend.
6. "We'll have to cut down costs if we want to improve our _____.", said Gregory at the meeting.
7. "Their company's _____ is located in Seattle.", said Jill to a coworker.
8. "I enjoy working with Mike. He's a real _____.", Tom told a coworker.

LISTEN & WRITE & ANSWER 9

TRACK 27

Write the questions you listen to and then choose the right answer:

1. _____?
- **a.** Sure, I think you should apply for that position.
- **b.** Yep, that's the applicant I told you about.
- **c.** Yes, I sure remember them.
- **d.** No, not yet, but we have an interview scheduled for three pm today.

2. _____?
- **a.** They sure enjoy working here.
- **b.** They're very gung-ho about their work.
- **c.** For just about a month. They're still getting into the swing of things.
- **d.** It should take them about fifteen minutes.

3. _____?
- **a.** That's what I like to do to enjoy myself.
- **b.** Yeah, I had a great time, thank you!
- **c.** I'll let you know when I find out.
- **d.** I really enjoy spending time with my family and going jogging.

4. _____?
- **a.** Sure, I've actually written a report on them. I'll e-mail it to you first thing when I get back to my office.
- **b.** I don't think he's qualified for this position.
- **c.** I'm sure they can handle this situation on their own.
- **d.** We need someone with a proactive profile.

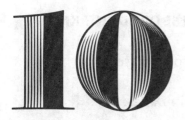

TRADE SHOWS
IS EVERYTHING ALL SET FOR THE HOUSTON FAIR?

🎧 TRACK 28

Barry: Hey, Fred, how's it going?

Fred: Great! I'm actually pretty excited about our new **product line**.

Barry: You do sound excited! Yeah, I agree completely. I feel like we can definitely win some serious **market share** with the new products we're launching.

Fred: Sure, and the **upcoming trade show** in Houston will be a great opportunity to **showcase** them.

Barry: True. By the way, is everything **all set** for the Houston fair?

Fred: Uh, pretty much so. We just need to **work out** some final details, but we should have everything **up and running** well ahead of time.

Barry: Sounds good. What about the new recruit? How's he getting along?

Fred: Pretty good, I mean, he's still **getting into the swing of things**, but he shows great potential and he's a fast learner.

Barry: I'm glad to hear that. That's really good news. Well, I have to get back to my office, I have a conference call with the regional managers in a few minutes. **Keep me posted** on the arrangements for the fair and let me know if you need any help.

Fred: Sure, Barry, I will. Thanks!

DIALOGUE COMPREHENSION – TRUE, FALSE OR I DON'T KNOW?

1. Barry thinks their market share is likely to increase.
   True ☐   False ☐   I don't know ☐
2. The upcoming trade show will take place in Dallas.
   True ☐   False ☐   I don't know ☐
3. Fred is the CFO of the company.
   True ☐   False ☐   I don't know ☐
4. The regional managers report to Barry.
   True ☐   False ☐   I don't know ☐

FOCUS ON WORDS & EXPRESSIONS

Find words or expressions in the dialogue that mean the same as:

a. Ready: _____

b. A group of products marketed by a company: _____

c. Happening soon; approaching: _____

d. Actively working; functioning: _____

e. Keep me informed: _____

f. The percentage of sales of a particular product held by a company: _____

g. Trade fair; a large event at which companies show their products to prospective customers: _____

h. Starting to understand how something works: _____

i. Find a solution; solve: _____

j. Show the best qualities of something: _____

THE CORPORATE WORLD – USUAL PHRASES AND QUESTIONS 10
TRACK 29

Do you know where the tech fair will take place this year?
I'll e-mail you the link to the fair website later.
We already have thirty-three exhibitors confirmed for the next trade show.
Have you already enrolled for the upcoming expo?
They plan to unveil their latest products at the annual trade show in L.A.
Which seminars do you plan to attend?
We'd better start planning ahead for the annual congress next year.
Do you plan to attend the upcoming trade fair in Dallas?
According to recent stats trade shows bring in about 20% of new clients.
On behalf of ABC International I'd like to welcome you all to our seventeenth annual convention.

CORPORATE ACRONYMS & ABBREVIATIONS 10

CIF = Cost Insurance Freight
Inc = Incorporated
Co = Company
memo = memorandum
no. = number

BUSINESS VOCABULARY & EXPRESSIONS 10

Match the words and expressions below to the definitions:

> 1. CALL OFF
> 2. BOOK
> 3. INTERNSHIP
> 4. UP IN THE AIR
> 5. HIT A SNAG
> 6. THINK BIG
> 7. FEASIBLE
> 8. WIN-WIN SITUATION

A. Uncertain; not yet decided. ( )
B. Possible; able to be done or achieved. ( )
C. A situation where both or all parties benefit from a deal. ( )
D. Cancel. ( )
E. Make a reservation; reserve. ( )
F. Run into an expected problem or difficulty. ( )
G. A job that a college student does for a short time in order to gain practical experience of a type of work. ( )
H. Set high goals; have big plans and ideas. ( )

GAP FILLING 10

Use the business vocabulary and expressions in the box to fill in the gaps in the sentences below:

> FEASIBLE   WIN-WIN SITUATION   THINK BIG   HIT A SNAG
> BOOK   INTERNSHIP   UP IN THE AIR   CALL OFF

1. "So, what's your take on Mike's action plan? Do you really think it sounds _____?", Roy asked Jake.
2. "Have you _____ any _____ with your current project so far?", Harry asked Nicholas at the meeting.
3. "We're working hard to try to reach a _____. We are doing our best to come to an agreement that will benefit all the parties.", said Mr. Clark.

4. "Any idea why they decided to _____ the meeting?", Gary asked a coworker.
5. "You shouldn't underestimate the market out there. You have to _____ if you want to make your new business grow.", Luke advised Ronald.
6. "As for the launch of the new product things are still _____. Our team is working out a few kinks so we don't know yet when we'll be able to finally release it.", Dave told Evelyn.
7. "Let's make sure we _____ the hotel rooms in advance. By the way, do you know any hotels close to the convention center?", Anderson asked Jill.
8. Doing an _____ is a great way to gain practical work experience.

LISTEN & WRITE & ANSWER 10

TRACK 30

Write the questions you listen to and then choose the right answer:

1. _____?
   a. Howard? Sure, I know who you're talking about.
   b. I might do that. Let's see how things play out.
   c. Yeah, I love this kind of event.
   d. I don't have a clue. I haven't talked to him in the past four days.

2. _____?
   a. Sure, I wish I could attend it too.
   b. No, I haven't read the program yet. Have you?
   c. I will, but I may show up a little late.
   d. Ok, we'll talk later then.

3. _____?
   a. It's huge, about 200 square meters, I guess.
   b. It's got a great design.
   c. The bigger the better, right?
   d. That's what I've been told.

4. _____?
  a. No, I haven't heard from him yet.
  b. Oh yeah, it was a great speech. I got a kick out of it!
  c. I know exactly what you mean.
  d. I'd love that.

ONLINE ADVERTISING
THEY SEEM TO BE INTERESTED IN OUR ONLINE CAMPAIGNS

TRACK 31

Barbara: Hey, Jeff, I'm curious. How was the meeting with that new **prospect** this morning?

Jeff: It was pretty good! I got the feeling that they're really interested in our creative online campaigns.

Barbara: Really? That's good news. So, would you say we **stand a fair chance** of getting a contract with them?

Jeff: I really think so. I felt like we could establish very good **rapport** with them and they want to schedule another meeting so we can **showcase** some recent campaigns we've done for our clients.

Barbara: Sounds great! I'm sure they'll be impressed with our ability to **come up with** innovative content for our campaigns. Any idea of how big their **advertising budget** is?

Jeff: They haven't given me a **ballpark figure** yet, but I guess I'll find out more about it next time I meet them. **For all I know** they've invested heavily in **billboards** and **TV spots** before. They seem to be interested in advertising in **social media** now.

Barbara: Great! I'm sure they know online advertising is our **expertise**.

Jeff: Yeah, I'm looking forward to our next meeting. By the way, have you seen Brian around?

Barbara: Yep, I talked to him briefly earlier today, but he's not in right now. He had a meeting with one of our current clients.

Jeff: Any idea when he should be back to the company?

Barbara: Uh, I think in the afternoon. Why?

Jeff: He said he wanted to talk to all of us about his new **brainchild**.

Barbara: Really? Brian is always full of bright ideas, I wonder what he's come up with this time.

Jeff: That's right! I guess we'll **find out** later today. Ok, Barbara, I **gotta** get back to my office and check my e-mail. Let me know when Brian is back.

Barbara: Sure, Jeff, I will!

DIALOGUE COMPREHENSION – TRUE, FALSE OR I DON'T KNOW?

1. Brian is attending a conference call in his office right now.
   True ☐   False ☐   I don't know ☐
2. Jeff had a very good first contact with their prospective client.
   True ☐   False ☐   I don't know ☐
3. Barbara thinks Brian is not a very creative person.
   True ☐   False ☐   I don't know ☐
4. Jeff needs to leave the office earlier today.
   True ☐   False ☐   I don't know ☐

FOCUS ON WORDS & EXPRESSIONS

Find words or expressions in the dialogue that mean the same as:

a. Large outdoor signboard: _____
b. Natural or acquired proficiency in a particular activity; ability; skill: _____
c. Rough estimate or figure: _____
d. Harmonious relationship: _____
e. A short section between TV programs used for advertising: _____
f. Potential customer: _____
g. The amount of money a company has available to spend on advertising: _____

h. Have a good chance: _____
i. Clever and original idea; invention; plan: _____
j. Show the best qualities of something: _____
k. Have to: _____
l. Websites that enable people to share content and engage in social networking: _____
m. Think of a plan, idea or solution: _____
n. Discover: _____
o. As far as I know: _____

THE CORPORATE WORLD – USUAL PHRASES AND QUESTIONS 11
🎧 TRACK 32

Our company's logo has been the same for the past ten years.
Have you visited that new prospect yet?
Will the commercial be broadcast during prime time?
They have come up with a very interesting online campaign.
How big is their advertising budget?
Two new web designers have been hired recently.
Do you have a good rapport with all your clients?
They made a killing selling those gadgets online.
We'll get better results if we focus on our target audience only.
Women play a major role in the workplace today.

CORPORATE ACRONYMS & ABBREVIATIONS 11

P.R. = Public Relations
CMO = Chief Marketing Officer
w/o = without
IOU = I Owe You
DBA = Doing Business As

BUSINESS VOCABULARY & EXPRESSIONS 11

Match the words and expressions below to the definitions:

1. BILLBOARD
2. GIMMICK
3. WINNER
4. LAUNCH
5. APPEAL
6. MARKET SHARE
7. PRIME TIME
8. INGENIOUS

A. The hours when television audiences are largest. ( )
B. Interest or attract someone. ( )
C. Very clever; innovative. ( )
D. The percentage of sales of a particular product held by a company. ( )
E. Large outdoor signboard. ( )
F. A marketing trick used to attract people's attention and interest. ( )
G. An event to introduce a new product. ( )
H. Something very popular or successful. ( )

GAP FILLING 11

Use the business vocabulary and expressions in the box to fill in the gaps in the sentences below:

| MARKET SHARE | INGENIOUS | APPEAL | PRIME TIME |
| WINNER | LAUNCH | BILLBOARD | GIMMICK |

1. "Have they already set a date for the official _____ of their new product?", Gary asked Jim.
2. "That was a clever publicity _____. Do you know who came up with that idea?", Brian asked a colleague.
3. "The advertising campaign will include TV spots and _____.", said Donovan at the meeting.
4. "I'm sure this new toy will be a _____. There's nothing like it in the market.", Mike told George.
5. "They expect to increase their _____ by at least 15% with their new product.", said Henry to a coworker.

68   ONLINE ADVERTISING

6. "I think our new gadget will _____ to both adults and the young crowd.", said Mark.
7. "Will the commercial be broadcast during _____?", Roger asked Norman.
8. "Jeff came up with an _____ idea for the marketing campaign.", Larry told Neil.

LISTEN & WRITE & ANSWER 11

TRACK 33

Write the questions you listen to and then choose the right answer:

1. _____?
   a. I don't know who is the official sponsor.
   b. Yeah, they've sponsored two events in the past few months.
   c. They might do that.
   d. I wish they would do that.

2. _____?
   a. It'll be great to share our experience with them.
   b. I wish I had a nine-to-five schedule like most of my friends.
   c. Not that I know of.
   d. My 10 am meeting has just been called off.

3. _____?
   a. It shouldn't take that long.
   b. Sure, I'll do that later.
   c. I think so.
   d. I think it looks great and modern. I really like it.

4. _____?
   a. Uh, I really think so. We've actually been getting good results.
   b. No, that's not my favorite social media website.
   c. It might be a good idea.
   d. They have a huge advertising budget.

A SHORT-STAFFED DEPARTMENT
THE WORKLOAD HAS BEEN INCREASING

🎧 TRACK 34

Hank: Have you seen Barry around?

Rachel: Uh, yeah, he's in the meeting room with Jake. Do you need to talk to him now?

Hank: I do. I need to confirm some details regarding our **booth** for the **upcoming trade fair** in Los Angeles.

Rachel: Uh, if I were you I'd wait a little. I heard him asking his secretary not to be disturbed. Anyway, he's been in the meeting room with Jake for over an hour now so I guess he should be **wrapping up** his meeting pretty soon.

Hank: Oh, thanks, Rachel! I can certainly wait. There's really **no rush**. So, I heard your department is **short-staffed**.

Rachel: That's right! The **workload** has been increasing considerably in the past few months, but things should go back to normal pretty soon. Martha will be returning to work from **maternity leave** next week.

Hank: That's good news. Have the people in your department been working **overtime** recently?

Rachel: Uh, some of them have as a matter of fact. Fortunately this is just a temporary situation.

Hank: Sure!

Rachel: Oh, I think Barry's available now.

Hank: Great! Thanks, Rachel, I'll talk to you later.

Rachel: Sure, bye!

DIALOGUE COMPREHENSION – TRUE, FALSE OR I DON'T KNOW?

1. Rachel prefers to leave home very early so she can beat the rush hour.
   True ☐   False ☐   I don't know ☐
2. Barry is having a meeting with Jake right now.
   True ☐   False ☐   I don't know ☐
3. Martha is pregnant.
   True ☐   False ☐   I don't know ☐
4. Hank needs to talk to Barry about their product line.
   True ☐   False ☐   I don't know ☐

FOCUS ON WORDS & EXPRESSIONS

Find words or expressions in the dialogue that mean the same as:

a. Trade show; a large event at which companies show their products to prospective customers: _____

b. A period of time a woman is legally allowed to be away from work in the weeks before and after she has a baby: _____

c. Extra hours that someone works in addition to their usual job hours: _____

d. A stand: _____

e. Finishing: _____

f. Happening soon; approaching: _____

g. The amount of work that a person has to do: _____

h. Without enough workers: _____

i. No hurry: _____

THE CORPORATE WORLD – USUAL PHRASES AND QUESTIONS 12
TRACK 35

This position requires someone with a proactive profile.
Where's the conference going to take place this year?
Do you have a high turnover of staff in your department?
We will have to work overtime to meet the deadline.
Lots of interesting ideas came up during our brainstorming session today.
Are you attending the upcoming trade show in Dallas?
Is everything all set for the trade fair in Chicago?
How was the meeting with the new supplier?
Do you know if that company offers internship programs?
You're doing a great job. Keep up the good work!

CORPORATE ACRONYMS & ABBREVIATIONS 12

POS = Point of Sale
VIP = Very Important Person
pls = please
LASER = Light Amplification by Stimulated Emission of Radiation
p.w. = per week

BUSINESS VOCABULARY & EXPRESSIONS 12

Match the words and expressions below to the definitions:

1. BLOCKBUSTER
2. FILL IN FOR
3. AFFORDABLE
4. PHASE OUT
5. RESILIENT
6. A DONE DEAL
7. TIME-CONSUMING
8. CALL IN SICK

A. That takes a long time to do. ( )

A SHORT-STAFFED DEPARTMENT

B. Call one's place of work to say you are ill and cannot come to work. ( )
C. A plan that has been arranged and that is now certain to happen. ( )
D. Something very successful with huge sales, esp. a movie or book. ( )
E. Not expensive. ( )
F. Substitute. ( )
G. Able to recover from difficulty; recovering quickly from adversity. ( )
H. Gradually stop manufacturing a product, etc. ( )

GAP FILLING 12

Use the business vocabulary and expressions in the box to fill in the gaps in the sentences below:

| TIME-CONSUMING | CALL IN SICK | RESILIENT | A DONE DEAL |
| AFFORDABLE | PHASE OUT | FILL IN FOR | BLOCKBUSTER |

1. "Seems like this new movie will be another _____.", Tracy told Laura.
2. That company _____ the old model of blender as soon as they released a new one.
3. "We may need to hire a marketing assistant to _____ Sheila while she's away on leave.", said Nick at the meeting.
4. "This is a very _____ task and I'm already swamped as it is. Do you think somebody else could take care of it?", Brian asked Gordon.
5. "Don't worry about him. He's very _____ and will bounce back in no time." , Bill told his friends.
6. "The merger is not _____ yet. They're still negotiating and trying to come to an agreement.", said Frank.
7. "Thank God I've always been very healthy. I've never had to _____.", Hank told Joe.
8. "I like coming to this shoe store because they usually have nice shoes and sneakers at _____ prices.", Tom told Jake.

THE WORKLOAD HAS BEEN INCREASING

LISTEN & WRITE & ANSWER 12

TRACK 36

Write the questions you listen to and then choose the right answer:

1. _____?
- **a.** Sure, that would be a lot easier.
- **b.** They have always been good providers.
- **c.** Yes, they do.
- **d.** Everything we need. I guess that's our best choice.

2. _____?
- **a.** Seems like they're on to something big.
- **b.** They play a major role in the marketplace.
- **c.** Something around 65%. They are market leaders as a matter of fact.
- **d.** I would say so.

3. _____?
- **a.** He comes to work by subway every day.
- **b.** He called in sick, but I don't know exactly what is the matter with him.
- **c.** I think he'll drop by later.
- **d.** He is not the kind of guy who would do something like that.

4. _____?
- **a.** I heard he got RSI from using his computer keyboard too long.
- **b.** He'll have to leave immediately.
- **c.** Yes, he is. He's leaving soon actually.
- **d.** He should know why that happened.

A DREAM JOB
WHAT IS IT LIKE?

TRACK 37

Rhonda: I heard you **landed** a dream job. So, tell me, what is it like?

Josh: Uh, well, I can't really complain, I mean, I've just been working at this new company for a couple of weeks, but I guess I can honestly say it feels great.

Rhonda: Good for you! What's the **compensation package** like? It must be pretty attractive, huh?

Josh: Yeah, the compensation package is quite generous as a matter of fact, it's actually above average if compared with companies in the same segment in the **marketplace**.

Rhonda: Sounds great! And the **perks**? I bet they offer great perks, don't they?

Josh: They do. They will even pay for **graduate school** once you've been with the company for over two years. But you know, I guess one of the best perks at this new company really is the informal environment and the friendly atmosphere.

Rhonda: I see, I guess people often **overlook** that, uh? So, is the **dress code** informal?

Josh: It is. Most people there wear casual clothes **on a daily basis**, even my director likes to dress informally.

Rhonda: I wonder if they have any **openings** right now, I have a friend who happens to be looking for a new opportunity and this company seems to be a great place to work.

Josh: I'll tell you what, I'm making a lot of friends there so I'll see if I can find out about new openings and I'll **keep you posted**.

Rhonda: That'd be great! Thanks, Josh!

Josh: You're welcome, Rhonda! Well, I have to **get going** now. Talk to you later.
Rhonda: Sure, Josh, take care!

DIALOGUE COMPREHENSION – TRUE, FALSE OR I DON'T KNOW?

1. The company where Josh works is looking for someone with advanced computer skills.
   True ☐   False ☐   I don't know ☐
2. Rhonda is looking for a new opportunity in the marketplace.
   True ☐   False ☐   I don't know ☐
3. Josh is very happy about his new job.
   True ☐   False ☐   I don't know ☐
4. The dress code where Josh works is formal.
   True ☐   False ☐   I don't know ☐

FOCUS ON WORDS & EXPRESSIONS

Find words or expressions in the dialogue that mean the same as:

a. Benefits beyond regular pay: _____
b. Fail to see or consider; ignore: _____
c. The world of business and commerce: _____
d. A set of rules specifying what you can wear for a particular occasion or place: _____
e. The salary and other benefits that an employee receives: _____
f. Every day: _____
g. Get something desirable such as a job or an opportunity: _____
h. A school in a university where students who already have a first degree can study for a master's degree or a doctorate: _____
i. Leave: _____
j. An available job or position: _____
k. Keep you informed: _____

A DREAM JOB

THE CORPORATE WORLD – USUAL PHRASES AND QUESTIONS 13
TRACK 38

The last two quarters were outstanding, we went beyond all our sales goals.
The new marketing manager gave us some useful tips about what to do when visiting customers.
How many active customers do you currently have on your database?
The whole project was the brainchild of our new sales director.
It takes most start-ups at least six months to just break even.
He's got a lot of experience and seems to know all the tricks of the trade.
The company's profits went up in the second quarter.
I wonder if they will okay our proposal.
It's about time we put our action plan into practice.
It seems like the project will finally get off the ground.

CORPORATE ACRONYMS & ABBREVIATIONS 13

GNP = Gross National Product
ERP = Enterprise Resources Planning
ATM = Automated Teller Machine
Co = Company
NPO = Non-Profit Organization; Not for Profit Organization

 BUSINESS VOCABULARY & EXPRESSIONS 13

Match the words and expressions below to the definitions:

1. RESIGN
2. GRAND OPENING
3. CURRENCY
4. RÉSUMÉ
5. GO PUBLIC
6. WORKFORCE
7. BONUS
8. ORGANIZATION CHART

WHAT IS IT LIKE?   77

A. A diagram showing the management structure of a company. ( )
B. Additional pay given to employee as incentive or reward. ( )
C. Sell shares of a privately owned company to the public. ( )
D. Money used in a particular country. ( )
E. Give up a job or position formally. ( )
F. Summary of one's academic qualifications and work experience. ( )
G. Official opening of a new business. ( )
H. The workers employed by a company. ( )

❋ GAP FILLING 13

Use the business vocabulary and expressions in the box to fill in the gaps in the sentences below:

BONUS	ORGANIZATION CHART	GO PUBLIC	WORKFORCE
CURRENCY	RÉSUMÉ	GRAND OPENING	RESIGN

1. About one third of the company's _____ was laid off as a result of the financial crisis.
2. "How many people do they plan to invite for the _____ of the new store?", Patty asked Dana.
3. The Australian dollar is the _____ in Australia.
4. "Have you heard the news? The head honcho promised us a _____ if we reach the sales goals for the quarter.", Louis told a coworker.
5. "I was not surprised when I heard Mario had _____ from the company since I knew he had plans to start his own business.", said Alex to a friend.
6. "That company seems to be doing really well since they _____.", Jim told a colleague.
7. "So, I see from your _____ that you have almost 5 years of managing experience. Can you tell me a little more about it?", the interviewer asked Jane.
8. The _____ of a company lays out exactly in what position each person is in each department.

78   A DREAM JOB

LISTEN & WRITE & ANSWER 13

TRACK 39

Write the questions you listen to and then choose the right answer:

1. _____?
- **a.** They've been doing it.
- **b.** He's planning to start a new company.
- **c.** We got two new clients recently, so things are looking up.
- **d.** Let's check and see what's going on there.

2. _____?
- **a.** There might be some openings right now.
- **b.** No, not really. We still need to take care of some details.
- **c.** It's been set for Thursday at 5 pm.
- **d.** That would be okay.

3. _____?
- **a.** They're currently importing from China.
- **b.** We spent about five hundred bucks there.
- **c.** I think you got a good deal.
- **d.** I have no idea. Why don't you ask Gregory? He might know.

4. _____?
- **a.** Sorry, I can't talk to you now, but Gary will tell you all about it.
- **b.** I don't like that game so much.
- **c.** We plan to visit them later today.
- **d.** No, it's not just a game people play.

WHAT IS IT LIKE?

OPENING A NEW BRANCH
LET'S TAKE ONE STEP AT A TIME

TRACK 40

Ralph: Hey, Liza, come on in!
Liza: Hi, Ralph. If you're busy I can come back later.
Ralph: Oh, no, please, come in. I really need to talk to you. Would you like something to drink?
Liza: Uh, yes, please, a **decaf**.
Ralph: Sure, let me get it for you.
Liza: Thanks! So, what did you want to talk to me about?
Ralph: Uh, as you know we've always had the intention of opening a new branch in Ohio.
Liza: Yes, sir. A branch in Ohio would be strategic according to our research.
Ralph: Ok, I guess I'd better just **cut to the chase** and ask you. How would the idea of **running** this new branch **appeal** to you?
Liza: Uh, gee, Ralph, are you serious? I mean, I think I wasn't prepared for this!
Ralph: I know. Sorry if I was too abrupt, you know me, I hate **beating around the bush**.
Liza: I'm actually pleased that you would consider me for such an important position, but I have to be honest, moving to Ohio would mean a huge change in my life and there are many aspects I would need to consider.
Ralph: I know exactly what you mean, that's why I'm asking you now. You will have **plenty** of time to **think it over**.
Liza: Any idea when this new branch should be **up and running**?

Ralph: It's gonna take **a long while**. As you know there are many arrangements we'll need to care of. We're talking about at least five to six months.

Liza: I see, well, I think I'm **overwhelmed** with this idea. I really appreciate your proposal.

Ralph: You deserve it! Ok, **let's take one step at a time**. I just want you to consider this possibility and let me know when you have your decision, **no rush**!

Liza: Thanks, Ralph!

DIALOGUE COMPREHENSION – TRUE, FALSE OR I DON'T KNOW?

1. They are planning to open a new branch in San Diego.
   True ☐ False ☐ I don't know ☐
2. Liza's main concern is her teenage daughter.
   True ☐ False ☐ I don't know ☐
3. Ralph does not put any pressure on Liza.
   True ☐ False ☐ I don't know ☐
4. Opening a new branch is a matter of weeks according to Ralph.
   True ☐ False ☐ I don't know ☐

FOCUS ON WORDS & EXPRESSIONS

Find words or expressions in the dialogue that mean the same as:

a. Actively working; functioning: _____

b. Managing; taking care of: _____
c. A large amount of something: _____

d. Interest or attract someone: _____
e. Decaffeinated coffee: _____
f. No hurry: _____
g. Say what is really important without delay; get to the point: _____

h. Not going straight to the point: _____

i. Struck by an intense emotional reaction: _____

j. Let's do things gradually, without rushing: _____

k. Consider something carefully: _____

l. A long time: _____

THE CORPORATE WORLD – USUAL PHRASES AND QUESTIONS 14
TRACK 41

Rachel was just getting into the swing of things when she was transferred to another department.
Have you had any feedback from customers about our new product line?
What's the retail price for this item?
Have those containers been inspected yet?
Our warehouse has about five hundred square meters of storage space.
Do you know when they'll be opening the new branch in Seattle?
Who's in charge of the logistics for this operation?
Wow, it sounds like a great proposal, but I'll have to think it over.
Can I sleep on it and give you my decision tomorrow?
Could you please just cut to the chase and tell me what's going on here?

CORPORATE ACRONYMS & ABBREVIATIONS 14

QC = Quality Control
VAT = Value Added Tax
PIN = Personal Identification Number
p.a. = per annum, per year
RSVP = Répondez S'il Vous Plaît, please reply

BUSINESS VOCABULARY & EXPRESSIONS 14

Match the words and expressions below to the definitions:

1. PAYROLL	5. DEMAND
2. INTRANET	6. END USER
3. THE PROS AND CONS	7. JET LAG
4. BOOM	8. TRADEMARK

A. The good and bad aspects of a situation; the advantages and disadvantages. ( )
B. The feeling of tiredness and confusion that people experience when crossing time zones during long flights. ( )
C. A registered name, symbol or design identifying a particular company. ( )
D. A list of employees and their salaries; the total amount of money paid to employees. ( )
E. The final user or consumer of a product. ( )
F. A private computer network that can be accessed only by the employees of a company. ( )
G. Grow rapidly. ( )
H. The amount of a product that customers want to buy. ( )

GAP FILLING 14

Use the business vocabulary and expressions in the box to fill in the gaps in the sentences below:

JET LAG	TRADEMARK	DEMAND	END USER
THE PROS AND CONS	BOOM	PAYROLL	INTRANET

1. "The company is doing very well. Business is _____ and we're all excited about the prospects.", said Nick to a friend.
2. Band-Aid, Kleenex and Lycra are well-known registered _____.

LET'S TAKE ONE STEP AT A TIME   83

3. "That company is growing fast. They have over 50 people on their _____ now and it seems the number keeps increasing all the time.", said Howard to a friend.
4. "They use the _____ to post important messages to the employees. It's actually very helpful.", Joe told Rita.
5. "We're planning to implement a night shift since _____ for our products is increasing.", the plant manager told Jake.
6. "Sorry, I was on a long flight and I haven't got over my _____ yet. I really need to rest for a while now.", Bob told Jill.
7. It's a lot easier to use that software now that they have come up with a friendly interface for the _____.
8. "They have been discussing _____ of opening a new branch on the west coast, but they haven't come to a consensus yet.", Brian told a coworker.

LISTEN & WRITE & ANSWER 14

TRACK 42

Write the questions you listen to and then choose the right answer:

1. _____?
   a. It's increased a little.
   b. It's quite a challenge.
   c. It's been out of sync.
   d. It got out of hand.

2. _____?
   a. The company's doing fine as a matter of fact.
   b. I think it's all a matter of time.
   c. I think he hasn't got over his jet lag yet.
   d. He's on a business trip to Japan.

3. _____?
   a. A guy named Howard Hughes, do you know him?
   b. He's been running about 5 miles a day.

OPENING A NEW BRANCH

c. We're running out of time.
   d. It's been open for just three days.

4. _____?
   a. The logistics for such a complex operation must be a challenge.
   b. I did. I talked to him over lunch yesterday.
   c. I think that's out of the question.
   d. No, I don't.

15

**BUSINESS GROWTH
THE SKY'S THE LIMIT!**

TRACK 43

Stacy: I heard your company got two new contracts recently.

Chris: That's right, I guess we're finally **reaping the rewards** of our hard work. Seems like things are really l**ooking up** for our company now.

Stacy: That's great! I bet your **sales reps** have been pretty busy then, uh? They must be making extra effort to just stay **on top of things**.

Chris: You're right! They definitely **have their hands full** right now, but the good thing is they're all very excited with the way things are going and the **prospects** for promotion are pretty encouraging to say the least.

Stacy: Cool! You do sound pretty **gung-ho** yourself. I guess motivation is everything, uh?

Chris: Sure, I'm really enthusiastic about this new phase. I sometimes can't believe that three **quarters** back we were having trouble reaching our sales goals. It's amazing how things have changed so fast for us.

Stacy: I see, you know, I've never really understood the corporate world. Seems like it's full of surprises! How did you guys manage to reverse the situation in such a short time?

Chris: Uh, well, we had to **instill** in our people the **crucial** steps we had to take in order to promote change. We've also implemented a series of measures making sure everyone knew what they were supposed to do so we could start moving towards a more favorable scenario.

Stacy: Sounds interesting.
Chris: Yeah, something else that's **played an important role** in overcoming our challenges is **teamwork**.
Stacy: Right! I've always heard teamwork is essential. So, what do you **envisage** happening now? I mean, do you see your company **moving to the next level**?
Chris: Sure! I'm pretty confident this is just the beginning. You know the saying, the sky's the limit!

DIALOGUE COMPREHENSION – TRUE, FALSE OR I DON'T KNOW?

1. Things at Christopher's company haven't always been the same as they are now.
   True ☐   False ☐   I don't know ☐
2. Christopher's company is planning to hire some new sales reps.
   True ☐   False ☐   I don't know ☐
3. Stacy has a good grasp of the corporate world.
   True ☐   False ☐   I don't know ☐
4. According to Christopher teamwork is crucial.
   True ☐   False ☐   I don't know ☐

FOCUS ON WORDS & EXPRESSIONS

Find words or expressions in the dialogue that mean the same as:

a. Extremely important: _____
b. A period of three months: _____
c. Cooperative effort done by a team in order to achieve a common goal: _____
d. The possibility of future success: _____
e. Had a big influence; was very important: _____
f. Imagine or expect something in the future: _____
g. Sales representatives: _____

h. Introduce an idea gradually into someone's mind: _____

i. Very enthusiastic or excited about something: _____

j. Improving or developing even more: _____

k. They are very busy: _____

l. Enjoying the results of something: _____

m. In control of what's happening: _____

n. Getting better; improving: _____

o. Great; nice: _____

THE CORPORATE WORLD – USUAL PHRASES AND QUESTIONS 15
TRACK 44

It's about time we took the company to the next level.
How important is teamwork in your opinion?
Teamwork plays a major role in building a business.
The past two quarters have been amazing. We reached all our sales goals.
Seems like we're now reaping the rewards of our efforts.
I'm really gung-ho about my job!
Things have been running smoothly in the past few months.
Business is booming and we're all excited about the prospects.
We've had record sales in the past two quarters.
Dividends will be distributed to all partners at the end of the year.

CORPORATE ACRONYMS & ABBREVIATIONS 15

ASAP = As Soon As Possible
FAQ = Frequently Asked Questions
EBITDA = Earning Before Interests, Taxes, Depreciation and Amortization
p.t.o. = please turn over
VP = Vice President

BUSINESS VOCABULARY & EXPRESSIONS 15

Match the words and expressions below to the definitions:

1. RETAIL	5. INVENTORY
2. CORPORATE LADDER	6. RESCHEDULE
3. FREEBIE	7. WHOLESALE
4. GOODS	8. MERGER

A. Items for sale; products. ( )
B. A list of all the items in stock; the process of updating such a list. ( )
C. The selling of goods to consumers; usually in small quantities and not for resale. ( )
D. Assign a new date for something to happen. ( )
E. Something given or received without charge, usually provided as part of a promotional scheme. ( )
F. The hierarchy of posts in a large corporation. ( )
G. The combination of two or more companies to form a bigger one. ( )
H. The selling of goods in large quantities to stores and businesses for resale to consumers. ( )

GAP FILLING 15

Use the business vocabulary and expressions in the box to fill in the gaps in the sentences below:

| RESCHEDULE | MERGER | WHOLESALE | INVENTORY |
| CORPORATE LADDER | GOODS | RETAIL | FREEBIES |

1. "We need to know the _____ price of this item so we can figure out how much we'll need to charge our customers.", Harry told Fred.
2. "Jeff has always been very ambitious. He actually started here as an intern and worked his way up the _____.", Margareth told Dave.

THE SKY'S THE LIMIT! 89

3. "They were giving some cool _____ at the grand opening of the new toy store downtown.", Celine told Rhonda.
4. "It will be a lot easier if we use a forklift to store the _____.", the plant manager told Doug.
5. "Do you know any good lawyers specializing in _____ acquisitions?", Tim asked a friend.
6. "Our marketing manager is on leave so I'm afraid we'll have to _____ the meeting with the sales reps for next week.", said Gregory.
7. "They are a big clothing company. They have over thirty _____ _____ outlets all over the U.S.", Jenny told a friend.
8. "Do you know how many items the _____ includes?", Jake asked Rachel.

LISTEN & WRITE & ANSWER 15

TRACK 45

Write the questions you listen to and then choose the right answer:

1. _____?
   a. He's a great lawyer.
   b. They specialize in acquisitions.
   c. Uh, let me think, yes, I think I know a good one.
   d. The new employees are informed about the company's policies regarding sexual harassment from day one.

2. _____?
   a. We'll have to reschedule it for sure.
   b. It's set for Thursday. Do you think you can make it?
   c. Uh, it seems one of the managers had a family emergency.
   d. Sure, the usual meeting point.

3. _____?
   a. We still need to pack the goods, remember?
   b. Their warehouse is huge.
   c. There's nothing we can do about it.
   d. I do hope so!

4. _____ ?
   a. It's written on that tag over there. Can you see it?
   b. No, that's the retail price.
   c. It's actually cheaper than the blue one.
   d. I guess so.

MANUFACTURING
PLANNING AHEAD IS ESSENTIAL

🔊 TRACK 46

Timothy: Hey, Eric, I've heard about the recent **bottlenecks** in production. How are things at the plant now?

Eric: Yeah, we've had some **kinks** to **work out**. Fortunately everything seems to be running **smoothly** now.

Timothy: I'm glad to hear that! What caused those bottlenecks anyway?

Eric: Uh, lack of **raw material** basically. One of our copper suppliers failed to deliver on time.

Timothy: I see, I do hope we don't **hit any more snags**. By the way, I have some good news, we've decided to buy four new **forklifts**.

Eric: Really? That's very good news, Tim. I'm pretty sure they'll help us speed things up around the **warehouse**. Any idea when they are due to arrive?

Timothy: I'd say by mid September. Uh, Eric, I was thinking, it might be a good idea to start researching other potential suppliers. Don't you think it might be risky to just depend on our current ones?

Eric: Sure, as a matter of fact we're doing that right now. I have a meeting with the representative of a new supplier company scheduled for next week.

Timothy: Great! **Planning ahead** is essential and you seem to be **on top of things**. **Congrats**! Keep up the good work.

DIALOGUE COMPREHENSION – TRUE, FALSE OR I DON'T KNOW?

1. Things are back on track at the plant now.
   True ☐ False ☐ I don't know ☐
2. Eric is planning to shut down the plant for maintenance soon.
   True ☐ False ☐ I don't know ☐
3. Timothy does not think Eric is doing a good job.
   True ☐ False ☐ I don't know ☐
4. The bottlenecks were caused by a lack of spare parts.
   True ☐ False ☐ I don't know ☐

FOCUS ON WORDS & EXPRESSIONS

Find words or expressions in the dialogue that mean the same as:

a. Run into unexpected problems or difficulties: _____

b. With no problems or difficulties: _____

c. In control of what is happening: _____

d. Problems in a part of a process that cause delays: _____

e. Small vehicles which have two metal bars fixed to the front used for lifting piles of goods: _____
f. Small problems: _____
g. Congratulations: _____
h. Find the solution to: _____

i. Make preparations or arrangements for the future: _____

j. Basic material used in manufacture: _____

k. A place for storage of goods: _____

l. Make something move or happen faster: _____

PLANNING AHEAD IS ESSENTIAL

THE CORPORATE WORLD – USUAL PHRASES AND QUESTIONS 16
TRACK 47

Can you walk me through the entire production process?
The recent bottlenecks in production have been caused by a lack of spare parts.
We may need to look for another copper supplier.
Can you show me some samples?
What can we do to minimize delays in the system?
We need to call a meeting to talk about the logistics of the operation.
Do all plant workers wear earplugs and goggles at all times?
How often are those machines lubricated?
Most of the raw material we use comes from China.
When are the new forklifts due to arrive?

CORPORATE ACRONYMS & ABBREVIATIONS 16

CAM = Computer-Aided Manufacturing
Lb = pound
RSI = Repetitive Strain Injury
JIT = Just In Time
K = thousand

BUSINESS VOCABULARY & EXPRESSIONS 16

Match the words and expressions below to the definitions:

1. OUTPUT	5. SAMPLE
2. IDLE TIME	6. GOGGLES
3. BLUE-COLLAR WORKER	7. ASSEMBLY LINE
4. EARPLUG	8. LOGISTICS

A. A device to protect the ears from loud noises. (   )
B. A system for manufacturing products in a factory, each worker

is responsible for a specific task which he repeats and then the process moves to the next worker and so on until the product is completely assembled and ready. ( )
C. The amount of something produced; goods or services produced by a company. ( )
D. A period during which a machine or employee is inactive. ( )
E. The planning and management of the details of an operation. ( )
F. Protective glasses. _____
G. Working class employee who performs manual or technical labor in a factory. ( )
H. Piece or item, such as of a product, that shows the quality of the whole. ( )

GAP FILLING 16

Use the business vocabulary and expressions in the box to fill in the gaps in the sentences below:

| BLUE-COLLAR WORKERS | GOGGLES | SAMPLE | IDLE TIME |
| ASSEMBLY LINE | OUTPUT | LOGISTICS | EARPLUG |

1. "The entire _____ planning process of such a complex operation must be very time-consuming.", said Bill to a coworker.
2. Despite their name, _____ don't always wear blue uniforms.
3. "I'll send you some free _____ so you can have a better idea of what our products look like.", said Ralph over the phone.
4. "I have no doubt that the new lubrication procedure will help us minimize the _____ of our machines.", said the plant manager at the meeting.
5. "It's really noisy at the plant. Make sure you wear _____ at all times.", Joe told a fellow worker.
6. "We have been able to increase our _____ by almost 25%, thanks to the new machines we imported from Japan.", the plant manager told a visitor.
7. _____ are usual in many different types of industries, but they are particularly associated with automobile

manufacturing. As a matter of fact, Henry Ford was one of the first entrepreneurs to introduce assembly lines in his manufacturing of automobiles.

8. "We had to run a series of workshops to get our plant workers to always wear earplugs and _____.", explained the plant manager to a visitor.

LISTEN & WRITE & ANSWER 16

🎧 TRACK 48

Write the questions you listen to and then choose the right answer:

1. _____?
a. Regular maintenance is crucial.
b. Things are running smoothly now.
c. I think once a week, but I'm not sure. Why don't you ask the plant manager?
d. The new procedure will help us speed up the process.

2. _____?
a. Two of them have been canceled.
b. No, not yet, but they should be shipped soon.
c. I'm not ready to order yet.
d. I think he works in the shipping department.

3. _____?
a. Uh, yeah, I'm sure we can come up with a tailor-made version that will fit your needs.
b. Yes, you can download it for free.
c. It takes a few days for the goods to be released from customs.
d. I think that's standard procedure.

4. _____?
a. The plant manager is on leave.
b. Just make sure you water the plants.
c. Sure, why not?
d. It's about 8% now, but it used to be higher.

MAKING PRESENTATIONS
I WAS WONDERING IF YOU COULD GIVE ME A FEW USEFUL TIPS

TRACK 49

Richard: Hey, Stephan, can I talk to you for a minute?
Stephan: Sure, Rick, come on in!
Richard: Thanks!
Stephan: So, **what have you been up to**?
Richard: Uh, a lot of things I guess. I've actually just started to **put together** my powerpoint presentation for the **talk** I'm supposed to give next month.
Stephan: Oh yeah? Is that what you wanted to talk to me about?
Richard: Exactly! You've always been so successful with your presentations that I was wondering if you could give me a few useful **tips**.
Stephan: Thanks for the **kind** words, Rick! You know, making a good presentation has a lot to do with feeling confident with the subject you will talk about, so take the time to create a script with good links from one point to the next and make sure your presentation flows naturally.
Richard: I see. What about visual aids, do you think using them can really make a presentation less **dull**?
Stephan: Definitely. Visual aids can certainly **brighten up** a speech and make it more dynamic, but ask yourself if a slide is really necessary before adding it. You don't want to overburden your **audience** with lots of pictures that are not relevant.
Richard: Good! I think I know what you mean. Now, what about the questions that the audience might ask, I'm always a little **concerned** that they might throw me some **curveballs,** you know.

Stephan: It's no use worrying, Rick. Just go over your script carefully and get prepared for any potential questions that could come up, and remember, you don't have to have the answer for every question, no one does! If you happen not to have the answer for a question you can always say you'll have to think more about it before coming to a conclusion. I have done that myself a couple of times.

Richard: Wow, thanks, Stephan, I think I'm feeling more confident now!

Stephan: I'm glad I can help. Ah, something else that's crucial, Rick: eye contact! Make sure you make eye contact with your audience, and don't talk too fast or too slow, but at a pace that keeps your audience **enticed**, always pausing before introducing a **key** point or topic.

Richard: Gee, Stephan, your tips have been **enlightening**! I don't know how I can thank you for such great advice.

Stephan: You're welcome, Rick. Like I said before, I'm really glad I can help. I'll tell you what, why don't you show me your script and slides when you're done?

Richard: Really? That'd be great!

Stephan: Good, so go back to your workstation now and keep working on it. I'm sure you're gonna come up with a great presentation.

DIALOGUE COMPREHENSION – TRUE, FALSE OR I DON'T KNOW?

1. Richard has never given a speech.
   True ☐   False ☐   I don't know ☐
2. Stephan thinks visual aids can be helpful.
   True ☐   False ☐   I don't know ☐
3. Richard isn't worried at all about the questions that the audience might ask him.
   True ☐   False ☐   I don't know ☐
4. In Stephan's opinion eye contact with the audience is extremely important.
   True ☐   False ☐   I don't know ☐

FOCUS ON WORDS & EXPRESSIONS

Find words or expressions in the dialogue that mean the same as:

a. Generous; pleasant; nice: _____
b. An informal lecture: _____
c. Worried: _____
d. Create something; organize something using different pieces or parts: _____
e. Boring; not interesting: _____
f. Attracted; interested: _____
g. What have you been doing? _____
h. Useful pieces of information or advice: _____
i. Tricky questions: _____
j. Make something more interesting or attractive: _____
k. Clarifying: _____
l. A group of listeners or spectators: _____
m. Important: _____

THE CORPORATE WORLD – USUAL PHRASES AND QUESTIONS 17
TRACK 50

Do you know who's making the keynote speech?
It was a great talk! He really seems to know his stuff.
The venue of the conference was great.
Who's giving the next talk?
Everyone seemed to enjoy the facilities of the place.
I was impressed with his presentation. He really gave me some food for thought.
Do you plan to attend the upcoming conference in Miami?
Where was the congress held last year?
Who's the keynote speaker?
That was a great session! I got a lot out of it.

CORPORATE ACRONYMS & ABBREVIATIONS 17

P.S. = Postscript
NLP = Neurolinguistic Programming
FDA = Food and Drug Administration
IMF = International Monetary Fund
B2B = Business to Business

 BUSINESS VOCABULARY & EXPRESSIONS 17

Match the words and expressions below to the definitions:

1. VENUE
2. BODY LANGUAGE
3. KEYNOTE SPEECH
4. ATTEND
5. HANDOUT
6. ON BEHALF OF
7. ENROLL
8. PRESS CONFERENCE

A. Be present at a meeting, lecture, etc. ( )
B. A piece of paper with information that is given to people attending a speech, lecture, etc. ( )
C. Place where a public event or meeting happens. ( )
D. Register formally as a participant of a lecture, show, etc. ( )
E. An interview in which a politician or famous person gives information to television reporters and answers questions. ( )
F. The gestures and facial expressions of someone that show what they are thinking or feeling. ( )
G. Speaking for; as a representative of. ( )
H. The main speech at an event. ( )

GAP FILLING 17

Use the business vocabulary and expressions in the box to fill in the gaps in the sentences below:

PRESS CONFERENCE	HANDOUT	ON BEHALF OF	ENROLL
BODY LANGUAGE	ATTEND	VENUE	KEYNOTE SPEECH

1. "It was a very interesting and dynamic lecture. I could tell from the speaker's _____ that he was feeling comfortable and confident.", Carol told Nick.
2. "_____ the organization committee I would like to welcome you to our twenty-first tech show.", announced an organization committee member at the convention center.
3. "There'll be some interesting talks at the tech expo. I've already _____ in three of them as a matter of fact.", said Lucy to a coworker.
4. To everyone's surprise the CEO of the company announced his resignation at a _____.
5. "A guy named Frank Williams from a company in Silicon Valley is making the _____ at the upcoming tech fair.", Celine told Daniel.
6. "I think this is an ideal _____ for our corporate conferences and meetings. It's got all the facilities we need.", Bill told Murray.
7. "Do you plan to _____ the sales seminar?", Ruth asked a coworker.
8. "Can you please help me distribute these _____ to the audience?", Mark asked Sally.

LISTEN & WRITE & ANSWER 17

TRACK 51

Write the questions you listen to and then choose the right answer:

1. _____?
a. She's really gung-ho about the new project.

- **b.** You've done a great job. Congrats!
- **c.** I think it was great. Her speech gave me some food for thought.
- **d.** Unfortunately I won't be able to attend it.

2. _____?
- **a.** Should I?
- **b.** Sure!
- **c.** Shall we?
- **d.** Oops, sorry!

3. _____?
- **a.** Oh yeah, I wouldn't miss it for the world.
- **b.** It's all about the new gadgets that are popping up.
- **c.** I think he's a great technician.
- **d.** I was actually impressed with the facilities of the venue.

4. _____?
- **a.** Yeah, I loved it. It was really good.
- **b.** I'm attending the conference.
- **c.** He's actually friends with the keynote speaker.
- **d.** Yeah, a guy named Gary Gordon. He's the CTO of a digital company in Silicon Valley.

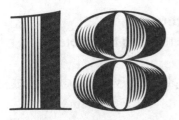

BUSINESS LUNCHES
I HATE TO TALK SHOP OVER MEALS!

 TRACK 52

Jonathan: Hey, Bart! How's it going?
Bart: Good! Do you mind if I sit here?
Jonathan: Of course not. **Be my guest**!
Bart: Thanks! Wow, I can't remember the last time I came to the company cafeteria.
Jonathan: Really? You've been out visiting clients a lot, haven't you?
Bart: Yeah, not just visiting clients, but on business lunches as well.
Jonathan: Business lunches? That's great. I wish I could **attend** some business lunches. I heard they take you guys out to some **snazzy** restaurants, right? I guess the food at these places must be great.
Bart: To tell you the truth I'm getting tired of all these business lunches.
Jonathan: Really? Why's that?
Bart: For one thing I hate **talking shop** over meals and I think we already have enough meetings at the company as it is, so I wish I could just enjoy lunch quietly.
Jonathan: I think I can understand what you mean. So, tell me, are these business lunches productive anyway?
Bart: Uh, I guess sometimes they are, but I don't think they are really necessary. The thing is my boss is a **confirmed** workaholic so he can't help talking business wherever he is. He'll talk shop even during happy hour, if you know what I mean.
Jonathan: Really? Seems like he's a workaholic beyond salvation!

Bart: That's right! I think **you got the picture**.
Jonathan: (laughing) Ok, Bart, I guess we'd better **drop the subject** and talk about something else now.
Bart: Right! Tell me about your weekend plans… (voice fading out)

DIALOGUE COMPREHENSION –TRUE, FALSE OR I DON'T KNOW?

1. Bart would rather not talk about work or business over lunch.
   True ☐   False ☐   I don't know ☐
2. Jonathan thinks attending business lunches must be cool.
   True ☐   False ☐   I don't know ☐
3. Bart has been going to the company cafeteria for lunch very often recently.
   True ☐   False ☐   I don't know ☐
4. Jonathan likes cooking.
   True ☐   False ☐   I don't know ☐

FOCUS ON WORDS & EXPRESSIONS

Find words or expressions in the dialogue that mean the same as:

a. You understood: _____

b. Having a particular habit or behavior; inveterate; not likely to change: _____

c. Go to an event such as a meeting, lecture, lunch, etc. _____

d. Talk about work or business during free time: _____

e. Stop talking about it: _____

f. Do as you wish; make yourself at home: _____

g. A self-service restaurant, often in a factory or an office building where people select their food and drink at a counter and take it to a table to eat: _____

h. Fashionable; modern and stylish: _____

THE CORPORATE WORLD – USUAL PHRASES AND QUESTIONS 18
TRACK 53

Do you have a spreadsheet with the breakdown of these figures?
We need to make sure expenditure will not exceed income.
I just came up with an amazing new idea to cut back on spending.
It sounds like a profitable investment. Can you tell me more about it?
There are good business opportunities in the franchise world.
Their company is opening a new branch overseas.
Make sure you know all the details before you dive into that project.
I think we should wrap up this meeting now.
We've had a hectic day. I think we all deserve some rest.
What do you say we call it a day?

CORPORATE ACRONYMS & ABBREVIATIONS 18

C/O = Care of
FOB = Free on Board
Inc = Incorporated
IRS = Internal Revenue Service
NYSE = New York Stock Exchange

BUSINESS VOCABULARY & EXPRESSIONS 18

Match the words and expressions below to the definitions:

1. STREAMLINE
2. MORALE
3. PARADIGM
4. FREE OF CHARGE
5. HANDS-ON
6. MICROMANAGE
7. BACK ON TRACK
8. MINDSET

A. According to schedule again. (   )
B. Way of thinking; mentality. (   )

I HATE TO TALK SHOP OVER MEALS!

C. Involving active participation; relating to practical experience. ( )
D. The amount of confidence and enthusiasm felt by a person or group of people. ( )
E. Simplify a process in order to increase its efficiency. ( )
F. Without any payment; for free. ( )
G. A model of something; a typical example or pattern of something. ( )
H. Manage or control a business or project with excessive attention to details. ( )

✱ GAP FILLING 18

Use the business vocabulary and expressions in the box to fill in the gaps in the sentences below:

| BACK ON TRACK | MINDSET | HANDS-ON | MICROMANAGE |
| PARADIGMS | FREE OF CHARGE | MORALE | STREAMLINE |

1. "I'm sure we can have this project _____ by the end of next week if we don't hit any more snags.", Sam told a coworker.
2. "My new boss is a real bean-counter. I think he _____ way too much.", said Ralph to a friend.
3. "You will only be able to break _____ if you think out of the box and approach tasks and problems in a different way than you usually do.", said Stanley to a group of managers.
4. "In my opinion they have a narrow-minded view of things. I really think they need to change their _____ if they want their company to grow.", said Tim at the meeting.
5. "For every item you buy in this section you get the second one _____.", explained the sales clerk at the department store.
6. "I love the new manager's proactive style. He's always trying to help us in every way. He's a _____ person.", said Rachel to a colleague.
7. "This new computer program should help us _____ our company's procedures and minimize our costs.", Gary told Richard.

8. "Seems like our employees' _____
definitely needs a boost. Any ideas on what we can do to reverse this situation?", asked Greg at the brainstorming session.

❁ LISTEN & WRITE & ANSWER 18

🎧 TRACK 54

Write the questions you listen to and then choose the right answer:

1. _____?
- **a.** Yeah, I've already smoked a pipe before.
- **b.** That's what I heard.
- **c.** It does, we actually have a lot of things going on these days.
- **d.** They work on the oil pipeline.

2. _____?
- **a.** Yeah, everything seems to be back on track now.
- **b.** Sure, I think everyone's here now.
- **c.** I wish we would have finished it before.
- **d.** I'm starting to believe it's really true after all.

3. _____?
- **a.** I doubt that could ever happen.
- **b.** That's great news!
- **c.** I agree, I think they have no morals.
- **d.** It's pretty high. Everyone seems to be excited about the new project.

4. _____?
- **a.** So far so good!
- **b.** Seems like they're reaping the rewards now.
- **c.** As a matter of fact I am.
- **d.** It sure feels like they're on a winning streak.

THE MERGER DEAL
SCENARIOS

🅟 TRACK 55

Max: Hi, Leslie. Have you talked to George about those **pending issues** yet?

Leslie: No, not yet. He's been **crazy busy** with the **merger** deal, so I'm waiting for the right moment to approach the subject with him.

Max: I see, I guess **we all have our hands full** with so many things **going on** these days. So, **what's your take** on the merger? Do you think it will really happen?

Leslie: **I don't have a clue**. All I know is they've been analyzing carefully **the pros and cons**. They want to make sure it would be beneficial for both parties.

Max: Sure, you know I'm not an **M&A** expert, but the way I see it there are two distinctive scenarios. A good one and a bad one.

Leslie: Really, now I'm curious, what are they?

Max: Well, the combined efforts of both companies would certainly create a stronger company, a market leader in the segment.

Leslie: Sure, joining forces would definitely help them win **market share**.

Max: Yeah, and their combined **expertis**e would make this new company unique and **unrivaled**.

Leslie: So, what's the bad scenario then?

Max: Uh, the **downside** is that unfortunately many people would eventually be fired. You see, many jobs would become **redundant** since the organizational structure is basically the same in each of the companies.

Leslie: **You have a point there**! That's what usually happens when two companies merge, right?
Max: Yep, I'm afraid so. Well, Leslie, I have to get back to my office and finish a report. I guess I'll see you later.
Leslie: Sure, Max, talk to you later!

DIALOGUE COMPREHENSION – TRUE, FALSE OR I DON'T KNOW?

1. Max is in charge of the merger deal.
   True ☐ False ☐ I don't know ☐
2. George is the CFO of the company.
   True ☐ False ☐ I don't know ☐
3. Leslie hasn't talked to George about some pending issues yet.
   True ☐ False ☐ I don't know ☐
4. There are a lot of things happening at Max and Leslie's company right now.
   True ☐ False ☐ I don't know ☐

FOCUS ON WORDS & EXPRESSIONS

Find words or expressions in the dialogue that mean the same as:

a. The percentage of sales of a particular product or products held by a company: _____
b. What's your opinion?: _____
c. Extremely busy: _____
d. Happening: _____
e. The advantages and disadvantages; the good and bad aspects of a situation: _____
f. Something that still needs to be dealt with: _____
g. We are all busy: _____
h. When two or more companies get together to form a bigger one: _____
i. Mergers and acquisitions: _____
j. Negative aspect of something; disadvantage: _____

SCENARIOS   109

k. I have no idea: _____
l. You are right; I agree with you: _____
m. Skill; ability; natural or acquired proficiency in a particular activity: _____
n. Unnecessary; not needed: _____
o. Incomparable; having no rival; better than any other of the same type: _____

THE CORPORATE WORLD – USUAL PHRASES AND QUESTIONS 19
TRACK 56

Richard is working on a complex merger deal.
What's the worst-case scenario if everything else goes wrong?
Have they fired any employees recently?
What are the pros and cons of the merger in your opinion?
There are some important issues we need to address in our weekly meeting.
What can we do to boost morale among the factory workers?
We need to hire someone with expertise in financial management.
The new policy will affect everyone across the board.
Can you tell me a little about the new projects in the pipeline?
We might make the wrong decision if we rush into things. Let's think it over.

CORPORATE ACRONYMS & ABBREVIATIONS 19

R&D = Reseach and Development
SWOT = Strengths, Weaknesses, Opportunities and Threats
qty = quantity
WTO = World Trade Organization
NASDAQ = National Association of Securities Dealers Automated Quotation

BUSINESS VOCABULARY & EXPRESSIONS 19

Match the words and expressions below to the definitions:

1. EMPOWER	5. DISRUPTION
2. PLAYER	6. BREAK EVEN
3. OUTSOURCE	7. ACROSS THE BOARD
4. WORST-CASE SCENARIO	8. MAKE A KILLING

A. An interruption in the usual way that something works; an act of delaying or interrupting the regular flow of something. ( )
B. The worst thing that could possibly happen. ( )
C. Have no profit or loss. ( )
D. Affecting everyone in a company or organization; applying to all members, groups or categories. ( )
E. Earn a lot of money quickly. ( )
F. Equip with an ability; enable. ( )
G. Influential person, company or organization, esp. in business or politics. ( )
H. Use a third-party service provider to execute a business function; obtain services from an outside supplier. ( )

GAP FILLING 19

Use the business vocabulary and expressions in the box to fill in the gaps in the sentences below:

ACROSS THE BOARD	MAKE A KILLING	DISRUPTION	BREAK EVEN
OUTSOURCE	WORST-CASE SCENARIO	EMPOWER	PLAYER

1. "Implementing a completely new procedure now is out of the question. It would cause a major _____ to our work schedule.", Benjamin told the others at the meeting.
2. "It seems that all business segments have been affected. The government has raised taxes _____.", Jerry told a colleague.

SCENARIOS 111

3. "How long do you think it will take that startup company to _____?", Jason asked a friend.
4. "They have cut costs by _____ their telemarketing to a specialized third-party service provider in India.", said Tim at the meeting.
5. "If we don't get the raw material we need from our suppliers in the next few days, we will have to delay deliveries to about one third of our customers. That would probably be the _____.", Harry told a coworker.
6. "When it comes to business the more you know about the corporate world the better, so I try to stay current with what the major _____ are doing, you know.", said Dick to a colleague.
7. "Wow, I'm really excited about the way things are going. Business is booming and I don't want to miss out on this opportunity to _____.", Steve told his partner.
8. "We'll only be able to grow faster and achieve better results if we _____ everyone on our staff.", said Will at the meeting.

❋ LISTEN & WRITE & ANSWER 19

🎧 TRACK 57

Write the questions you listen to and then choose the right answer:

1. _____?
a. The way I see it, everything is changing so fast.
b. Sure, I don't want to be stuck in a dead-end job for the rest of my life.
c. It can be a pretty boring job after a while.
d. No, I haven't applied for that job yet.

2. _____?
a. I find that empowering.
b. That would be the worst-case scenario for us.
c. I try to stay current with what's going on in the corporate world.
d. It may take a while, but I really think it will happen.

3. _____?
   a. Not yet, but I'm working on it.
   b. Sure, let's talk business.
   c. Yes, I've seen it before.
   d. That's a great business plan.

4. _____?
   a. I don't really think so. I can only see advantages.
   b. It could surely be beneficial to all parties.
   c. That's one of the upsides.
   d. It might be a good idea.

CORPORATE SCANDAL
HOW COULD A RESPECTFUL AND CLEVER EXECUTIVE GET INTO THIS?

TRACK 58

Dylan: Hey, Ron, do you have a minute?
Ronald: Sure, **what's up**?
Dylan: I have some **first-hand** news about the recent corporate scandal.
Ronald: Do you? Have you been talking to someone?
Dylan: Yeah, I **ran into** Nick at Joe's Diner, and you know, he has some **inside information** about what's been going on lately. It seems that the recent **findings** are just the **tip of the iceberg**.
Ronald: Really? Wow, I still find it hard to believe that their financial director would do something like that.
Dylan: I know, he'd always been considered above suspicion, uh?
Ronald: That's right. How could a respectful and clever executive get into this?
Dylan: Clever, uh? Maybe too clever! Not only did he steal money from the company, but also **masterminded** one of the biggest corruption scandals that's ever been heard of.
Ronald: So, what else did Nick tell you?
Dylan: Nick thinks that he'll definitely **face charges**.
Ronald: Do you think he might **be charged with embezzlement**?
Dylan: I think that's likely to happen. You see, the evidence is pretty **overwhelming**.
Ronald: Has he said anything in his defense yet?
Dylan: Yeah, he's denied any **wrongdoing** so far, but that's what all the **crooks** say right?
Ronald: Wow, seems like you can't trust anyone anymore.
Dylan: That's right!

DIALOGUE COMPREHENSION – TRUE, FALSE OR I DON'T KNOW?

1. Ronald is not at all interested in the recent corporate scandal.
   True ☐   False ☐   I don't know ☐
2. Dylan often has lunch at Joe's Diner.
   True ☐   False ☐   I don't know ☐
3. According to Nick the scandal has not been completely unveiled yet.
   True ☐   False ☐   I don't know ☐
4. The financial director involved in the scandal had always had an impeccable reputation.
   True ☐   False ☐   I don't know ☐

FOCUS ON WORDS & EXPRESSIONS

Find words or expressions in the dialogue that mean the same as:

a. Very great or strong: _____
b. Small part of a problem that is really much larger: _____
c. Theft of funds placed in one's trust: _____
d. Coming directly from the original source: _____
e. Secret information about an organization: _____
f. What's going on?; what's the matter?: _____
g. Be officially accused of committing a crime: _____
h. Plan and organize a complex operation, often a crime: _____
i. Meet or find someone by chance: _____
j. Illegal or dishonest behavior: _____
k. Information that is discovered as a result of investigation: _____
l. Be accused of: _____
m. Criminals; thieves: _____

HOW COULD A RESPECTFUL AND CLEVER EXECUTIVE GET INTO THIS?

THE CORPORATE WORLD – USUAL PHRASES AND QUESTIONS 20
TRACK 59

The financial director of the company was accused of embezzlement.
They decided to patent the invention immediately to make sure it was protected.
Do you think they will file a lawsuit against that company for damages?
That company has been charged with tax evasion before.
It was a very complex trial. The jury took five hours to reach a verdict.
Everyone deserves a fair trial despite what they have done.
The case will be tried in a competent court of law.
Can we sue them for breach of contract?
Has that company been sued for damages before?
Do you know any good law firm that could take care of this for us?

CORPORATE ACRONYMS & ABBREVIATIONS 20

IPO = Initial Public Offering
B2C = Business to Consumer
DOB = Date of Birth
EC = European Community
OPEC = Organization of the Petroleum Exporting Countries

BUSINESS VOCABULARY & EXPRESSIONS 20

Match the words and expressions below to the definitions:

1. TAX HAVEN
2. SUE
3. LOAN SHARK
4. LAWSUIT
5. LAUNDER
6. SWINDLE
7. TRIAL
8. SCAM

116   CORPORATE SCANDAL

A. Obtain money dishonestly from a person or a company. ( )
B. A fraudulent business scheme, a dishonest plan for making money. ( )
C. Take legal action against a person or organization; file a lawsuit against. ( )
D. Hearing and judgment of a matter in a court of law. ( )
E. A country, state or independent region where taxes are low. ( )
F. Convert illegally obtained funds into legal ones. ( )
G. Someone who lends money at excessive rates of interest. ( )
H. A legal proceeding in a court of law involving a claim, complaint, etc. ( )

GAP FILLING 20

Use the business vocabulary and expressions in the box to fill in the gaps in the sentences below

SCAM	LOAN SHARK	TRIAL	SWINDLE
LAUNDER	SUE	TAX HAVEN	LAWSUIT

1. "Do you think they might file a _____ against us?", Roger asked his partner.
2. Switzerland is one of the most popular _____. The tax rates there are low and the country has highly reputable banks.
3. "That politician you told me about seems to be involved in a lot of shady deals. I read in the paper that he's been recently accused of money _____.", George told a friend.
4. "I know a guy who got into a lot of trouble when he borrowed money from a _____. If I were you I'd really avoid doing it.", Ralph advised Jake.
5. "The two directors were found to be involved in the scam. It seems that they _____ the company out of $ 200,000.", Joe told a coworker.
6. The lawyer warned Jim that if he went ahead with the accusations they might _____ him for damages.
7. The ex-CFO of the company is scheduled to stand _____ for fraud next month.

8. "It seems that the crooks made loads of money with the insurance _____.", Fred told a friend.

❋ LISTEN & WRITE & ANSWER 20

🔊 TRACK 60

Write the questions you listen to and then choose the right answer:

1. _____?
a. He'll have plenty of time to rest in jail now.
b. That's what crooks and scumbags usually do.
c. Seriously? That guy should be behind bars.
d. He stole taxpayer money. That's why he's in jail now.

2. _____?
a. He's been accused of embezzlement.
b. That's a good question. I don't think he has so many friends now.
c. I think he's up to no good.
d. He made loads of money with that scam.

3. _____?
a. Not yet.
b. It's been a complex trial.
c. The plaintiff did.
d. Yes, one of the witnesses had done it.

4. _____?
a. They could certainly do that.
b. That's how they plan to raise funds.
c. They plan to raise money for the project through crowdfunding.
d. They're going to make a killing with their new app.

Answer Key

1

A HECTIC SCHEDULE
WORKING OVERTIME TO MEET DEADLINES

Dialogue comprehension – True, False or I don't know?
1. False
2. True
3. I don't know
4. False

Focus on words & expressions
a. workload
b. overtime
c. head honcho
d. hectic
e. meet the deadline
f. burnout
g. pulling my leg
h. grab a bite
i. recruit
j. cafeteria
k. workstation
l. tough it out

Business vocabulary & expressions 1
A. Core business
B. Call it a day
C. Swamped (with work)
D. Absenteeism
E. Run a business
F. Behind schedule
G. Bossy
H. Twenty-four seven

Gap filling 1
1. Some convenience stores in big urban centers are open **twenty-four seven**.
2. "As you know we are **behind schedule** with our current project. I think we'll have to put in some extra work over the next few days.", said the general manager to his team.
3. "Our strategy has always been to focus on our **core business** and outsource our non-core activities.", said George at the meeting.
4. I don't like working with the new regional manager because he's way too **bossy**.

ANSWER KEY 119

5. "Sorry, I can't talk to you right now. I'm **swamped** with work.", Dave told a friend over the phone.
6. "We've done enough work for today. Let's **call it a day**.", Bill told a coworker.
7. Mr. Drake Jr. has been **running** the family **business** since his father passed away.
8. "What can employers do to reduce **absenteeism** rates in the workplace?

Listen & Write & Answer 1
1. How long is your commute to work?
   c. About twenty minutes.
2. What's the deadline for our current project?
   b. September, 15th, but don't worry, we're ahead of schedule.
3. Do you get along with all your coworkers?
   d. Oh yeah, they're all very friendly.
4. Where's your company's headquarters?
   a. It's in Houston.

CORPORATE RELATIONSHIPS
A CONFLICT WITH THE NEW REGIONAL MANAGER

Dialogue comprehension – True, False or I don't know?
1. False
2. True
3. I don't know
4. True

Focus on words & expressions
a. micromanaging
b. breathing down my neck
c. control freak
d. bugging
e. corporate culture
f. plain
g. getting it off your chest
h. is something the matter?
i. wisely

120   TALKING BUSINESS

Business vocabulary & expressions 2

A. Call the shots
B. Eager beaver
C. In charge of
D. Peer
E. Laid-back
F. Play hardball
G. Demanding
H. Boss around

Gap filling 2

1. "I need to talk to the person **in charge of** accounts payable please.", said Mr. Smith over the phone.
2. "Is your new boss very **demanding**?", Carla asked a friend.
3. "The new manager has a very aggressive style. I don't think he will put up with **laid-back** employees.", said Martha to a coworker.
4. Some people believe you have to **play hardball** to move up the corporate ladder.
5. "If you want to talk business you have to see Nicholas. He's the one who **calls the shots** around here.", said Dave to the newcomer.
6. "I wish you would stop **bossing me around**.", said Jill to a coworker.
7. Ronald seems to have a good rapport with his **peers**.
8. The new sales rep gets to work early every morning. He's a real eager beaver.

Listen & Write & Answer 2

1. What's the dress code like where you work?
    c. It's pretty casual and I like it that way.
2. Why don't you tell me what's bugging you?
    b. Uh, OK, maybe I'd better get it off my chest.
3. Do you have a good rapport with the new director?
    d. I do. We get along fine.
4. What's the new sales manager like?
    a. He's demanding, but he's also very considerate and supportive.

3

BUSINESS AS USUAL
PUTTING OUT FIRES AT WORK!

Dialogue comprehension – True, False or I don't know?
1. True
2. I don't know
3. True
4. False

Focus on words & expressions
a. recharge one's batteries
b. short-staffed
c. booming
d. workload
e. ASAP
f. Put out fires
g. hire
h. on leave
i. rough
j. prospects
k. casual Friday
l. perks
m. quarter
n. at ease
o. peer
p. other than that

Business vocabulary & expressions 3
A. Highlights
B. Red tape
C. Teamwork
D. Staff
E. At stake
F. All set
G. On duty
H. Game plan

Gap filling 3
1. "You have to have a **game plan** for your career if you want to move up the corporate ladder.", said Sean to a friend.
2. "Jeff works for a small company with a **staff** of just over twenty employees.", Hank told Monica.
3. "I'll be **on duty** from noon to nine pm today.", said Don to a friend.
4. "Can you brief me on the **highlights** of the conference?", Gary asked a coworker.
5. "Some of the applicants interviewed this week showed great **teamwork** skills.", said the human resources manager to a coworker.
6. "I wish there was a way to cut through the **red tape** and speed up the process.", said Richard to a coworker.
7. "We'd better call a meeting ASAP and try to come up with a

solution to this problem. There's a lot **at stake** here.", Mr. Gordon told his team.
8. "Is everything **all set** for the presentation tomorrow morning?", Howard asked Melanie.

Listen & Write & Answer 3
1. Why has the meeting been called off?
   c. I don't have a clue.
2. Do you think the clothes people wear reflect on their mood?
   a. I have no doubt about it. The work environment does feel more relaxing when people are dressed casually.
3. Does your company have an intranet?
   d. Sure, all important news and messages are posted on the intranet. It's very useful.
4. How's the company doing?
   b. Pretty good. We've reached all our sales goals for the past three quarters.

A NEW SUPPLIER
I GOOGLED THEM AND GUESS WHAT I FOUND OUT?

Dialogue comprehension – True, False or I don't know?
1. True
2. I don't know
3. False
4. True

Focus on words & expressions
- **a.** head honcho
- **b.** set up a meeting
- **c.** I don't have a clue
- **d.** e-mail someone
- **e.** wrap it up
- **f.** competitor
- **g.** sales rep
- **h.** spreadsheet
- **i.** grab a bite
- **j.** ASAP
- **k.** google
- **l.** cafeteria
- **m.** take a rain check
- **n.** swamped with work

Business vocabulary & expressions 4
A. Plan ahead
B. Purchase
C. Workaholic
4. Call a meeting
5. Facilities
6. On top of things
7. Bail out
8. Day off

Gap filling 4
1. "Larry likes to be **on top of things** so we'd better keep him posted.", said Brian at the meeting.
2. The company is headquartered in a high-tech office building offering all kinds of modern **facilities**.
3. The marketing manager plans to **call a meeting** soon to talk about the new product line.
4. Mr. Dickson hardly ever goes on vacation. He's also the first one to arrive in the office and the last one to leave. He's a confirmed **workaholic**.
5. "Where can we **purchase** that kind of machine?", Jason asked Robin.
6. "They may have to close down the business if no one **bails** them **out**.", said Howard to his friends.
7. "I like to go jogging in the park and get a tan on my **day off**.", said Michael to a coworker.
8. When it comes to business it's always good to **plan ahead**.

Listen & Write & Answer 4
1. What's the current status of the project?
    d. Things are running smoothly. We'll surely meet the deadline, don't worry!
2. Have you had any feedback from customers about the new product?
    c. The response has been very positive so far, but we still need to wait a little longer.
3. Do you think we might be able to gain some market share with this new strategy?
    a. Definitely. We have a great game plan and I'm sure it's going to work just fine.
4. What's your take on that new product?
    d. I think that new toy is great. I've never seen anything like that, honestly, I think it will be a hit with the kids.

THE BOARD MEETING
HAVE YOU BEEN EAVESDROPPING ON THEM?

Dialogue comprehension – True, False or I don't know?
1. False
2. True
3. False
4. I don't know

Focus on words & expressions
a. beforehand
b. intranet
c. Nope
d. eavesdropping
e. you have attended
f. cubicle
g. drop the subject
h. wrap up
i. first-hand

Business vocabulary & expressions 5
A. Crunch numbers
B. Plummet
C. Stats
D. Ballpark figure
E. Set up shop
F. Shift
G. Take a toll on
H. By the book

Gap filling 5
1. "I heard they **set up shop** back in the early 70's, with a small office in New Jersey.", said Luke to a friend.
2. The accountants have been **crunching numbers** all day trying to figure out if it's worth replacing the old machines for new ones.
3. According to the **stats** demand for this kind of product has been increasing.
4. Working eleven hours a day is starting **to take a toll** on Ronald.
5. "Can you give me a **ballpark figure** on how much you're planning to spend?", Jake asked Ronald.
6. "How many people work on the night **shift**?", Harry asked the plant manager.
7. "Seems like stock prices have **plummeted** again today.", Fred told a friend.
8. "I was really surprised when I heard about that company's shady deals since they had always done everything **by the book**.", said Barry to a coworker.

ANSWER KEY   125

Listen & Write & Answer 5
1. How much are you willing to invest in this new project?
   b. As much as necessary, I do believe this is crucial to us.
2. Would you consider working on the night shift?
   d. No, I could never do that. I don't think it's healthy.
3. Have any sales reps been hired recently?
   a. No, but we may need to hire a new one soon.
4. Do you have any idea how much that new equipment would cost the company?
   c. Uh, I think five thousand dollars is a good ballpark figure.

TECHNOLOGY
HEADING TOWARDS ANOTHER BIG REVOLUTION YET!

Dialogue comprehension – True, False or I don't know?
1. True
2. False
3. False
4. I don't know

Focus on words & expressions
a. gadgets
b. massive
c. sci-fi
d. someday
e. app
f. you can say that again
g. 3D printing
h. ingenious
i. bound to
j. heading towards

Business vocabulary & expressions 6
A. Flash drive
B. Cutting-edge
C. Hacker
D. Trend
E. Tablet
F. Start-up
G. Silicon Valley
H. Geek

Gap filling 6
1. "I'm sure our visitors will love our high-tech plant and the **cutting-edge** technology of our machines.", said Brian to a coworker.

126   TALKING BUSINESS

2. "When it comes to business, keeping updated on the latest market **trends** is crucial.", Walter told Jim.
3. "We've been invited to visit a high-tech company in **Silicon Valley** next week. I'm really excited about it.", said Josh to a friend.
4. "How long do you think it will take that **start-up** to break even?", Frank asked Elizabeth.
5. "Hey, Charlie, do you know any **geeks** who might be able to help me out with this new computer system?", Jeff asked Roy.
6. "We'd better back up all these files. Can you pass me that **flash drive** please?", Roger asked a coworker.
7. "This new **tablet** is likely to do well in the gadget market.", said Hank to a coworker.
8. "Apparently a **hacker** broke into the company's computer system and altered some of the information. They're still trying to figure out what happened.", Rachel told a friend.

Listen & Write & Answer 6
1. What's the wifi password please?
   c. It's greatbreakcafe 123.
2. Have you deleted any names from that list?
   b. Uh, sorry! I may have done that by mistake.
3. Do you need a printout of this letter?
   a. Not really. The digital version will do.
4. Do you think that new gadget will catch on?
   d. I'm sure it will. I think it will be a hit with the young crowd.

INNOVATION
THINKING OUT OF THE BOX

Dialogue comprehension – True, False or I don't know?
1. True
2. I don't know
3. False
4. False

Focus on words & expressions
a. highlights
i. call a meeting

- **b.** plays a key role
- **c.** branch office
- **d.** brainstorming
- **e.** gotta
- **f.** bright
- **g.** think out of the box
- **h.** come up with
- **j.** bold
- **k.** fit in
- **l.** product line
- **m.** make of
- **n.** narrow-minded
- **o.** I'm looking forward to it

Business vocabulary & expressions 7
- **A.** Pricy
- **B.** Networking
- **C.** Office supplies
- **D.** Suck you dry
- **E.** Holding company
- **F.** So far so good
- **G.** Take time of
- **H.** Small talk

Gap filling 7
1. "I really need to **take time off** and relax. I've been feeling stressed out lately.", said Hank to a coworker.
2. "The upcoming trade show in Vegas will be a good opportunity to do some **networking**.", said Dave to a coworker.
3. "We're running low on some **office supplies**. Can you buy some A4 paper and staples next time you go to the stationery store?", Gordon asked Nick.
4. "I can't afford to go to **pricy** restaurants right now.", said Jeff to a friend.
5. "Do you enjoy making **small talk** with strangers at parties?", Phillip asked Norman.
6. "If I were you I'd go easy on the slot machines. They can **suck you dry** you know.", Charlie advised Greg.
7. "A **holding company** doesn't really engage in any operations itself. It basically owns stocks of the companies it controls.", explained Donald at the meeting.
8. Barry: "So, Mike, how's your new job?"
   Mike: "**So far so good**, I've only been there for a week now, but I'm really enjoying it.".

Listen & Write & Answer 7
1. So, what's the game plan for this new project?
   - **b.** I don't have a clue, but I think we'll find out soon enough. The marketing director has called a meeting to talk about it.

2. Do you know if they offer internship programs?
   d. They do. I actually met one of their interns a couple of weeks ago.
3. Can you put me through to Mr. Hopper's secretary?
   a. Sure, sir, hold on a second, I'll transfer your call.
4. Does casual Friday apply to the plant workers as well?
   c. No, unfortunately not. I think the factory guys would love to dress casually at least once a week, but they have to wear a uniform every day.

THE NEW GADGET
A PARADIGM SHIFT!

Dialogue comprehension – True, False or I don't know?
1. I don't know
2. False
3. True
4. True

Focus on words & expressions
a. feasible
b. at the cutting-edge
c. appeal
d. the clock is ticking
e. timeline
f. features
g. prospects
h. up and running
i. gadget
j. a hit
k. you nailed it!
l. state-of-the-art
m. you can say that again
n. haste makes waste
o. you have a point
p. pal
q. hitting the shelves
r. paradigm shift

Business vocabulary & expressions 8
A. Spreadsheet
B. Ups and downs
C. In the pipeline
D. Out of the question
E. Budget
F. Touch base with
G. Tricks of the trade
H. Ahead of schedule

Gap filling 8
1. "They've been in this business for such a long time that I'm sure they know all the **tricks of the trade**."
2. "Can you e-mail the financial **spreadsheet** to me later?", Kurt asked Jill.
3. The sales manager travels to San Francisco twice a month to **touch base with** the sales people at the branch office there.
4. "That company you told me about is an active player in the market. Seems like they have lots of projects **in the pipeline**.", said Joe to a coworker.
5. "Buying a new machine now is **out of the question**. We simply can't afford it now.", said the financial manager at the meeting.
6. "This is a very competitive market so there will always be **ups and downs** in business, my friend.", said the manager to the new recruit.
7. "Apparently they run their business on a very tight **budget**.", said Bill to a friend.
8. "Fortunately we're **ahead of schedule** and will surely meet the deadlines for our current projects.", said Burt to a coworker.

Listen & Write & Answer 8
1. Do you know how this app works?
    a. No, I'm not familiar with it yet.
2. Do you use any social networking websites?
    c. We do. We often use LinkedIn. It's designed specifically for the business community.
3. So, what was your first impression of their products?
    b. I had a good first impression, but I need to learn more about them.
4. Is everything all set for the launch?
    d. Yep, everything's ready, don't worry!

HIRING THE RIGHT PEOPLE
HAVE YOU MET THE NEW RECRUITS YET?

Dialogue comprehension – True, False or I don't know?
1. True
2. I don't know
3. False
4. True

Focus on words & expressions
a. cafeteria
b. hear through the grapevine
c. recruit
d. a bunch of
e. early bird
f. bright
g. grabbing a bite to eat
h. yep
i. rush hour

Business vocabulary & expressions 9
A. Bottom line
B. Headquarters
C. Competitive edge
D. Team player
E. In a nutshell
F. Kink
G. Gung-ho
H. Start from scratch

Gap filling 9
1. "I'm glad everyone seems to be **gung-ho** about our new project. Motivation is everything!", said the marketing director.
2. "We have a few **kinks** to work out with this project, but I'm sure it will be a very successful one.", Nick told a coworker.
3. "Sorry, I don't have time for long explanations now. Can someone give me the facts **in a nutshell**?"
4. Knowing how to speak other languages can certainly give you a **competitive edge** when looking for a job.
5. "You mean they have built a solid company in just about two years and now hire 72 people? Can you believe they actually **started from scratch**?", Donald asked a friend.
6. "We'll have to cut down costs if we want to improve our **bottom line**.", said Gregory at the meeting.
7. "Their company's **headquarters** is located in Seattle.", said Jill to a coworker.

ANSWER KEY 131

8. "I enjoy working with Mike. He's a real **team player**.", Tom told a coworker.

Listen & Write & Answer 9
1. Have you interviewed any applicants today?
   d. No, not yet, but we have an interview scheduled for three pm today.
2. How long have they been with the company?
   c. For just about a month. They're still getting into the swing of things.
3. What are you favorite leisure time activities?
   d. I really enjoy spending time with my family and going jogging.
4. Can you tell me a little about the profile of the applicants interviewed so far?
   a. Sure, I've actually written a report on them. I'll e-mail it to you first thing when I get back to my office.

TRADE SHOWS
IS EVERYTHING ALL SET FOR THE HOUSTON FAIR?

Dialogue comprehension – True, False or I don't know?
1. True
2. False
3. I don't know
4. True

Focus on words & expressions
a. all set
b. product line
c. upcoming
d. up and running
e. keep me posted
f. market share
g. trade show
h. getting into the swing of things
i. work out
j. showcase

Business vocabulary & expressions 10
A. Up in the air
B. Feasible
C. Win-win situation
D. Call off
E. Book
F. Hit a snag
G. Internship
H. Think big

132   TALKING BUSINESS

Gap filling 10

1. "So, what's your take on Mike's action plan? Do you really think it sounds **feasible**?", Roy asked Jake.
2. "Have you hit any **snags** with your current project so far?", Harry asked Nicholas at the meeting.
3. "We're working hard to try to reach a **win-win situation**. We are doing our best to come to an agreement that will benefit all the parties.", said Mr. Clark.
4. "Any idea why they decided to **call off** the meeting?", Gary asked a coworker.
5. "You shouldn't underestimate the market out there.
You have to **think big** if you want to make your new business grow.", Luke advised Ronald.
6. "As for the launch of the new product things are still **up in the air**. Our team is working out a few kinks so we don't know yet when we'll be able to finally release it.", Dave told Evelyn.
7. "Let's make sure we **book** the hotel rooms in advance.   By the way, do you know any hotels close to the convention center?", Anderson asked Jill.
8. Doing an **internship** is a great way to gain practical work experience.

Listen & Write & Answer 10

1. Do you know if Howard has already enrolled for the upcoming trade show?
   d.   I don't have a clue. I haven't talked to him in the past four days.
2. Have you decided which talks you want to attend?
   b.   No, I haven't read the program yet. Have you?
3. How big is their booth?
   a.   It's huge, about 200 square meters, I guess.
4. Did you enjoy the keynote speech?
   b.   Oh yeah, it was a great speech. I got a kick out of it!

ONLINE ADVERTISING
THEY SEEM TO BE INTERESTED IN OUR ONLINE CAMPAIGNS

Dialogue comprehension – True, False or I don't know?
1. False
2. True
3. False
4. I don't know

Focus on words & expressions
a. billboard
b. expertise
c. ballpark figure
d. rapport
e. TV spot
f. prospect
g. advertising budget
h. stand a fair chance
i. brainchild
j. showcase
k. gotta
l. social media
m. come up with
n. find out
o. for all I know

Business vocabulary & expressions 11
A. Prime time
B. Appeal
C. Ingenious
D. Market share
E. Billboard
F. Gimmick
G. Launch
H. Winner

Gap filling 11
1. "Have they already set a date for the official **launch** of their new product?", Gary asked Jim.
2. "That was a clever publicity **gimmick**. Do you know who came up with that idea?", Brian asked a colleague.
3. "The advertising campaign will include TV spots and **billboards**.", said Donovan at the meeting.
4. "I'm sure this new toy will be a **winner**. There's nothing like it in the market.", Mike told George.
5. "They expect to increase their **market share** by at least 15% with their new product.", said Henry to a coworker.
6. "I think our new gadget will **appeal** to both adults and the young crowd.", said Mark.

134 TALKING BUSINESS

7. "Will the commercial be broadcast during **prime time**?", Roger asked Norman.
8. "Jeff came up with an **ingenious** idea for the marketing campaign.", Larry told Neil.

Listen & Write & Answer 11
1. Has that company ever sponsored any events?
   b. Yeah, they've sponsored two events in the past few months.
2. Has the meeting with the advertising agency been scheduled yet?
   c. Not that I know of.
3. So, what's your take on their new logo?
   d. I think it looks great and modern. I really like it.
4. Do you think social media advertising works?
   a. Uh, I really think so. We've actually been getting good results.

A SHORT-STAFFED DEPARTMENT
THE WORKLOAD HAS BEEN INCREASING

Dialogue comprehension – True, False or I don't know?
1. I don't know
2. True
3. False
4. False

Focus on words & expressions
a. trade fair
b. maternity leave
c. overtime
d. booth
e. wrapping up
f. upcoming
g. workload
h. short-staffed
i. no rush

Business vocabulary & expressions 12
A. Time-consuming
B. Call in sick
C. A done deal
D. Blockbuster
E. Affordable
F. Fill in for
G. Resilient
H. Phase out

ANSWER KEY   135

Gap filling 12
1. "Seems like this new movie will be another **blockbuster**.", Tracy told Laura.
2. That company **phased out** the old model of blender as soon as they released a new one.
3. "We may need to hire a marketing assistant to **fill in for** Sheila while she's away on leave.", said Nick at the meeting.
4. "This is a very **time-consuming** task and I'm already swamped as it is. Do you think somebody else could take care of it?", Brian asked Gordon.
5. "Don't worry about him. He's very **resilient** and will bounce back in no time.", Bill told his friends.
6. "The merger is not **a done deal** yet. They're still negotiating and trying to come to an agreement.", said Frank.
7. "Thank God I've always been very healthy. I've never had to **call in sick**.", Hank told Joe.
8. "I like coming to this shoe store because they usually have nice shoes and sneakers at **affordable** prices.", Tom told Jake.

Listen & Write & Answer 12
1. What kind of facilities does that convention center provide?
   d. Everything we need. I guess that's our best choice.
2. How big is their market share?
   c. Something around 65%. They are market leaders as a matter of fact.
3. Why isn't Brian coming to work today?
   b. He called in sick, but I don't know exactly what is the matter with him.
4. Do you know why Bill is on leave?
   a. I heard he got RSI from using his computer keyboard too long.

13

A DREAM JOB
WHAT IS IT LIKE?

Dialogue comprehension – True, False or I don't know?
1. I don't know
2. False
3. True
4. False

Focus on words & expressions
a. perks
b. overlook
c. marketplace
d. dress code
e. compensation package
f. on a daily basis
g. land
h. graduate school
i. get going
j. opening
k. keep you posted

Business vocabulary & expressions 13
A. Organization chart
B. Bonus
C. Go public
D. Currency
E. Resign
F. Résumé
G. Grand opening
H. Workforce

Gap filling 13
1. About one third of the company's **workforce** was laid off as a result of the financial crisis.
2. "How many people do they plan to invite for the **grand opening** of the new store?", Patty asked Dana.
3. The Australian dollar is the **currency** in Australia.
4. "Have you heard the news? The head honcho promised us a **bonus** if we reach the sales goals for the quarter.", Louis told a coworker.
5. "I was not surprised when I heard Mario had **resigned** from the company since I knew he had plans to start his own business.", said Alex to a friend.
6. "That company seems to be doing really well since they **went public**.", Jim told a colleague.
7. "So, I see from your **résumé** that you have almost 5 years of managing experience. Can you tell me a little more about it?", the interviewer asked Jane.

8. The **organization chart** of a company lays out exactly in what position each person is in each department.

Listen & Write & Answer 13
1. How's the company doing now?
    c. We got two new clients recently, so things are looking up.
2. Is everything all set for the grand opening?
    b. No, not really. We still need to take care of some details.
3. What's the currency in Taiwan?
    d. I have no idea. Why don't you ask Gregory? He might know.
4. So, do you have a game plan for this new project?
    a. Sorry, I can't talk to you now, but Gary will tell you all about it.

OPENING A NEW BRANCH
LET'S TAKE ONE STEP AT A TIME

Dialogue comprehension – True, False or I don't know?
1. False
2. I don't know
3. True
4. False

Focus on words & expressions
a. up and running
b. running
c. plenty
d. appeal
e. decaf
f. no rush
g. cut to the chase
h. beating about the bush
i. overwhelmed
j. let's take one step at a time
k. think it over
l. a long while

Business vocabulary & expressions 14
A. The pros and cons
B. Jet lag
C. Trademark
D. Payroll
E. End user
F. Intranet
G. Boom
H. Demand

138 TALKING BUSINESS

Gap filling 14

1. "The company is doing very well. Business is **booming** and we're all excited about the prospects.", said Nick to a friend.
2. Band-Aid, Kleenex and Lycra are well-known registered **trademarks**.
3. "That company is growing fast. They have over 50 people on their **payroll** now and it seems the number keeps increasing all the time.", said Howard to a friend.
4. "They use the **intranet** to post important messages to the employees. It's actually very helpful.", Joe told Rita.
5. "We're planning to implement a night shift since **demand** for our products is increasing.", the plant manager told Jake.
6. "Sorry, I was on a long flight and I haven't got over my **jet lag** yet. I really need to rest for a while now.", Bob told Jill.
7. It's a lot easier to use that software now that they have come up with a friendly interface for the **end user**.
8. "They have been discussing **the pros and cons** of opening a new branch on the west coast, but they haven't come to a consensus yet.", Brian told a coworker.

Listen & Write & Answer 14

1. Has demand for your products increased at all in the past few months?
    a. It's increased a little.
2. What's the matter with Joe?
    c. I think he hasn't got over his jet lag yet.
3. Who's running the new store?
    a. A guy named Howard Hughes, do you know him?
4. Do you know who's in charge of logistics there?
    d. No, I don't.

ANSWER KEY

15

BUSINESS GROWTH
THE SKY'S THE LIMIT!

Dialogue comprehension – True, False or I don't know?
1. True
2. I don't know
3. False
4. True

Focus on words & expressions
a. crucial
b. quarter
c. teamwork
d. prospects
e. played an important role
f. envisage
g. sales reps
h. instill
i. gung-ho
j. moving to the next level
k. have their hands full
l. reaping the rewards
m. on top of things
n. looking up
o. cool

Business vocabulary & expressions 15
A. Goods
B. Inventory
C. Retail
D. Reschedule
E. Freebie
F. Corporate ladder
G. Merger
H. Wholesale

Gap filling 15
1. "We need to know the **wholesale** price of this item so we can figure out how much we'll need to charge our customers.", Harry told Fred.
2. "Jeff has always been very ambitious. He actually started here as an intern and worked his way up the **corporate ladder**.", Margareth told Dave.
3. "They were giving some cool **freebies** at the grand opening of the new toy store downtown.", Celine told Rhonda.
4. "It will be a lot easier if we use a forklift to store the **goods**.", the plant manager told Doug.
5. "Do you know any good lawyers specializing in **mergers** and acquisitions?", Tim asked a friend.
6. "Our marketing manager is on leave so I'm afraid we'll have to

reschedule the meeting with the sales reps for next week.", said Gregory.
7. "They are a big clothing company. They have over thirty **retail** outlets all over the U.S.", Jenny told a friend.
8. "Do you know how many items the **inventory** includes?", Jake asked Rachel.

Listen & Write & Answer 15
1. Do you know any lawyers specializing in mergers?
   c. Uh, let me think, yes, I think I know a good one.
2. Do you know why they rescheduled the meeting?
   c. Uh, it seems one of the managers had a family emergency.
3. Is there enough space to store all the goods in our warehouse?
   d. I do hope so!
4. What's the wholesale price of this item please?
   a. It's written on that tag over there. Can you see it?

16
MANUFACTURING
PLANNING AHEAD IS ESSENTIAL

Dialogue comprehension – True, False or I don't know?
1. True
2. I don't know
3. False
4. False

Focus on words & expressions
a. hit snags
b. smoothly
c. on top of things
d. bottlenecks
e. forklifts
f. kinks
g. congrats
h. work out
i. plan ahead
j. raw material
k. warehouse
l. speed up

Business vocabulary & expressions 16
A. Earplug
B. Assembly line
E. Logistics
F. Goggles

C. Output
D. Idle time
G. Blue-collar worker
H. Sample

Gap filling 16
1. "The entire **logistics** planning process of such a complex operation must be very time-consuming.", said Bill to a coworker.
2. Despite their name, **blue-collar workers** don't always wear blue uniforms.
3. "I'll send you some free **samples** so you can have a better idea of what our products look like.", said Ralph over the phone.
4. "I have no doubt that the new lubrication procedure will help us minimize the **idle time** of our machines.", said the plant manager at the meeting.
5. "It's really noisy at the plant. Make sure you wear **earplugs** at all times.", Joe told a fellow worker.
6. "We have been able to increase our **output** by almost 25% thanks to the new machines we imported from Japan.", the plant manager told a visitor.
7. **Assembly lines** are usual in many different types of industries, but they are particularly associated with automobile manufacturing. As a matter of fact, Henry Ford was one of the first entrepreneurs to introduce assembly lines in his manufacturing of automobiles.
8. "We had to run a series of workshops to get our plant workers to always wear earplugs and **goggles**.", explained the plant manager to a visitor.

Listen & Write & Answer 16
1. How often do they shut down the plant for maintenance?
    c. I think once a week, but I'm not sure. Why don't you ask the plant manager?
2. Have the orders been shipped yet?
    b. No, not yet, but they should be shipped soon.
3. Can the software be customized to fit our needs?
    a. Uh, yeah, I'm sure we can come up with a tailor-made version that will fit your needs.
4. Is the turnover high with the people at the plant?
    d. It's about 8% now, but it used to be higher.

17
MAKING PRESENTATIONS
I WAS WONDERING IF YOU COULD GIVE ME A FEW USEFUL TIPS

Dialogue comprehension – True, False or I don't know?
1. I don't know
2. True
3. False
4. True

Focus on words & expressions
a. kind
b. talk
c. concerned
d. put together
e. dull
f. enticed
g. what have you been up to?
h. tips
i. curveballs
j. brighten up
k. enlightening
l. audience
m. key

Business vocabulary & expressions 17
A. Attend
B. Handout
C. Venue
D. Enroll
E. Press conference
F. Body language
G. On behalf of
H. Keynote speech

Gap filling 17
1. "It was a very interesting and dynamic lecture. I could tell from the speaker's **body language** that he was feeling comfortable and confident.", Carol told Nick.
2. "**On behalf of** the organization committee I would like to welcome you to our twenty-first tech show.", announced an organization committee member at the convention center.
3. "There'll be some interesting talks at the tech expo. I've already **enrolled** in three of them as a matter of fact.", said Lucy to a coworker.
4. To everyone's surprise the CEO of the company announced his resignation at a **press conference** .
5. "A guy named Frank Williams from a company in Silicon Valley is making the **keynote speech** at the upcoming tech fair.", Celine told Daniel.

ANSWER KEY   143

6. "I think this is an ideal **venue** for our corporate conferences and meetings. It's got all the facilities we need.", Bill told Murray.
7. "Do you plan to **attend** the sales seminar?", Ruth asked a coworker.
8. "Can you please help me distribute these **handouts** to the audience?", Mark asked Sally.

Listen & Write & Answer 17
1. So, did you like the marketing manager's presentation?
   c. I think it was great. Her speech gave me some food for thought.
2. Can you help me give out these handouts to the audience please?
   b. Sure!
3. Are you attending the upcoming tech show?
   a. Oh yeah, I wouldn't miss it for the world.
4. Do you know who's making the keynote speech?
   d. Yeah, a guy named Gary Gordon. He's the CTO of a digital company in Silicon Valley.

18

BUSINESS LUNCHES
I HATE TO TALK SHOP OVER MEALS!

Dialogue comprehension – True, False or I don't know?
1. True
2. True
3. False
4. I don't know

Focus on words & expressions
a. you got the picture
b. confirmed
c. attend
d. talk shop
e. drop the subject
f. be my guest
g. cafeteria
h. snazzy

Business vocabulary & expressions 18
A. Back on track
B. Mindset
C. Hands-on
D. Morale
E. Streamline
F. Free of charge
G. Paradigm
H. Micromanage

144 TALKING BUSINESS

Gap filling 18

1. "I'm sure we can have this project **back on track** by the end of next week if we don't hit any more snags.", Sam told a coworker.
2. "My new boss is a real bean-counter. I think he **micromanages** way too much.", said Ralph to a friend.
3. "You will only be able to break **paradigms** if you think out of the box and approach tasks and problems in a different way than you usually do.", said Stanley to a group of managers.
4. "In my opinion they have a narrow-minded view of things. I really think they need to change their **mindset** if they want their company to grow.", said Tim at the meeting.
5. "For every item you buy in this section you get the second one **free of charge**.", explained the sales clerk at the department store.
6. "I love the new manager's proactive style. He's always trying to help us in every way. He's a **hands-on** person.", said Rachel to a colleague.
7. "This new computer program should help us **streamline** our company's procedures and minimize our costs.", Gary told Richard.
8. "Seems like our employees' **morale** definitely needs a boost. Any ideas on what we can do to reverse this situation?", asked Greg at the brainstorming session.

Listen & Write & Answer 18

1. Does your company have any other projects in the pipeline?
    - **c.** It does, we actually have a lot of things going on these days.
2. Shall we get started then?
    - **b.** Sure, I think everyone's here now.
3. How's morale in the office?
    - **d.** It's pretty high. Everyone seems to be excited about the new project.
4. How are things going for you on your current project?
    - **a.** So far so good!

19
THE MERGER DEAL
SCENARIOS

Dialogue comprehension – True, False or I don't know?
1. False
2. I don't know
3. True
4. True

Focus on words & expressions
a. market share
b. what's your take?
c. crazy busy
d. going on
e. the pros and cons
f. pending issue
g. we all have our hands full
h. merger
i. M&A
j. downside
k. I don't have a clue
l. you have a point there
m. expertise
n. redundant
o. unrivaled

Business vocabulary & expressions 19
A. Disruption
B. Worst-case scenario
C. Break even
D. Across the board
E. Make a killing
F. Empower
G. Player
H. Outsource

Gap filling 19
1. "Implementing a completely new procedure now is out of the question. It would cause a major **disruption** to our work schedule.", Benjamin told the others at the meeting.
2. "It seems that all business segments have been affected. The government has raised taxes **across the board**.", Jerry told a colleague.
3. "How long do you think it will take that startup company to **break even**?", Jason asked a friend.
4. "They have cut costs by **outsourcing** their telemarketing to a specialized third-party service provider in India.", said Tim at the meeting.
5. "If we don't get the raw material we need from our suppliers in the next few days, we will have to delay deliveries to about one third of our customers. That would probably be the **worst-case scenario**.

6. "When it comes to business the more you know about the corporate world the better, so I try to stay current with what the major **players** are doing, you know.", said Dick to a colleague.
7. "Wow, I'm really excited about the way things are going. Business is booming and I don't want to miss out on this opportunity to **make a killing**.", Steve told his partner.
8. "We'll only be able to grow faster and achieve better results if we **empower** everyone on our staff.", said Will at the meeting.

Listen & Write & Answer 19
1. Have you thought about changing jobs?
    b. Sure, I don't want to be stuck in a dead-end job for the rest of my life.
2. Do you really think that deal will go through?
    d. It may take a while, but I really think it will happen.
3. Have you come up with a business plan yet?
    a. Not yet, but I'm working on it.
4. Are there any downsides to this strategy?
    a. I don't really think so. I can only see advantages.

CORPORATE SCANDAL
HOW COULD A RESPECTFUL AND CLEVER EXECUTIVE GET INTO THIS?

Dialogue comprehension – True, False or I don't know?
1. False
2. I don't know
3. True
4. True

Focus on words & expressions
a. overwhelming
b. the tip of the iceberg
c. embezzlement
d. first-hand
e. inside information
f. what's up?
g. face charges
h. mastermind
i. run into
j. wrongdoing
k. findings
l. be charged with
m. crooks

Business vocabulary & expressions 20
A. Swindle
B. Scam
C. Sue
D. Trial
E. Tax haven
F. Launder
G. Loan shark
H. Lawsuit

Gap filling 20
1. "Do you think they might file a **lawsuit** against us?", Roger asked his partner.
2. Switzerland is one of the most popular **tax havens**. The tax rates there are low and the country has highly reputable banks.
3. "That politician you told me about seems to be involved in a lot of shady deals. I read in the paper that he's been recently accused of money **laundering**.", George told a friend.
4. "I know a guy who got into a lot of trouble when he borrowed money from a **loan shark**. If I were you I'd really avoid doing it.", Ralph advised Jake.
5. "The two directors were found to be involved in the scam. It seems that they **swindled** the company out of $ 200,000.", Joe told a coworker.
6. The lawyer warned Jim that if he went ahead with the accusations they might **sue** him for damages.
7. The ex-CFO of the company is scheduled to stand **trial** for fraud next month.
8. "It seems that the crooks made loads of money with the insurance **scam**.", Fred told a friend.

Listen & Write & Answer 20
1. Why has he been arrested?
   d. He stole taxpayer money. That's why he's in jail now.
2. Do you think someone will bail him out?
   b. That's a good question. I don't think he has so many friends now.
3. Has the jury reached a verdict yet?
   a. Not yet.
4. How are they going to finance the project?
   c. They plan to raise money for the project through crowdfunding.

Glossary

A

3D printing: the process of making a physical object from a three-dimensional digital model
A4 paper: paper in the A series frequently used in offices
A bunch of: a group of
A done deal: a plan that has been arranged and that is now certain to happen
A hit: something very successful
A lack of: absence of
A long while: a long time
Absenteeism: the state of being absent from work
Accounts payable: money owed by a company to its creditors
Across the board: affecting everyone in a company or organization; applying to all members, groups or categories.
Advertising budget: the amount of money a company has available to spend on advertising
Affordable: not expensive
AGM: Annual General Meeting
Ahead of schedule: done earlier than the expected time
All set: ready
A.M.: Ante Meridiem, before noon
Amazing: very surprising
App: an application (computer program) especially one designed for a mobile device
Appeal/appealed/appealed: engage the attention and interest of
Applicant: candidate
Arrest/arrested/arrested: take into legal custody; detain
ASAP: As Soon As Possible
Assembly line: a system for manufacturing products in a factory, each worker is responsible for a specific task which he repeats and then the process moves to the next worker and so on until the product is completely assembled and ready

ATM: Automated Teller Machine
Attend/attended/attended: go to an event such as a meeting, lecture, lunch, etc
At stake: at risk; in danger of being lost
At the cutting-edge: at the most advanced stage of something
At the forefront: the leading or most important position; the position of greatest advancement
Audience: a group of listeners or spectators

B2B: Business to Business
B2C: Business to Consumer
Background: someone's previous experience or training
Back on track: according to schedule again
Bail out: help a company or someone out of a difficult situation, often by giving them money; set someone who is arrested free by paying bail
Ballpark figure: rough estimate or figure
Bean counter: too concerned with numbers and details
Beating about the bush: not going straight to the point
Be charged with: be accused of
Beforehand: in advance
Behind schedule: running late
Be my guest: do as you wish; make yourself at home
Billboard: large outdoor signboard
Blender: an electrical appliance used in the kitchen that mixes food ingredients, blends liquids, etc.
Blockbuster: something very successful with huge sales, esp. a movie or book
Blue-collar worker: working class employee who performs manual or technical labor in a factory
Board meeting: a meeting of the board of directors of a company
Body language: the gestures and facial expressions of someone that show what they are thinking or feeling.
Bold: courageous; brave; fearless and daring
Bonus: additional pay given to employee as incentive or reward
Book/booked/booked: make a reservation; reserve

Boom/boomed/boomed: grow rapidly
Boost: an increment in amount, number or volume; an increase
Boost/boosted/boosted: increase; raise
Booth: a stand
Bossy: tending to give orders to others; authoritarian
Boss around: give orders, esp. in an unpleasant way; keep telling someone what to do
Bother/bothered/bothered: annoy; disturb
Bottleneck: a problem in a part of a process that causes delays
Bottom line: the most important thing to consider; the end result
Bounce back: recover, become hopeful and enthusiastic again, usually after an unpleasant experience such as an illness
Bound to: certain or destined to
Brainchild: clever and original idea; invention; plan
Brainstorming: a problem-solving technique in which members of a group spontaneously contribute ideas and suggestions
Branch office: an office representing a company in a particular area
Breach of contract: failure to live up to the terms of a contract
Breakdown: when a machine stops working; a division of something into smaller parts
Break even: make neither profit nor loss
Breathe down one's neck: put pressure on someone; watch someone closely
Bright: intelligent
Brighten up: make something more interesting or attractive
Broadcast/broadcast/broadcast: transmit programs on radio or television
BTW: By The Way
Budget: the amount of money a company has available to spend
Bug/bugged/bugged: annoy
Burnout: physical or emotional exhaustion as a result of prolonged stress or overwork
By the book: according to the rules

CAD: Computer-Aided Design
Cafeteria: a self-service restaurant, often in a factory or an office building

where people select their food and drink at a counter and take them to a table to eat
Call a meeting: schedule a meeting
Call in sick: call one's place of work to say you are ill and cannot come to work
Call it a day: declare an end to the day's activities; end a day's work
Call off/called off/called off: cancel
Call the shots: give orders; make the decisions
CAM: Computer-Aided Manufacturing
Casual Friday: a working day on which it is acceptable to dress casually at work
Catch on: become popular
Catch up on: do something that you have not been able to do recently
CEO: Chief Executive Officer
CFO: Chief Financial Officer
CIF: Cost Insurance Freight
Co: Company
COD: Cash On Delivery
Come up with: think of a plan, idea, solution, etc
Commute: the trip to and from work
Commute/commuted/commuted: travel from one's home to one's workplace and vice versa
Compensation package: the salary and other benefits that an employee receives
Competitive edge: clear advantage over the competition
Competitor: a company that sells the same products or services as another company
Concern: worry
Concerned: worried
Confirmed: having a particular habit or behavior; inveterate; not likely to change
Congrats: congratulations
Considerate: showing concern for the feelings and needs of other people; kind and helpful
Control freak: someone with an obsessive need to exert control over situations and people
C/O: Care Of
COO: Chief Operating Officer

Cool: nice; great; trendy
Copper: a red-brown metal used for making pipes, wire and coins
Core business: a company's main activity
Corporate culture: the values, behavior and dress code of a corporation
Corporate ladder: the hierarchy of posts in a large corporation
CPA: Certified Public Accountant
CPU: Central Processing Unit
Crazy busy: extremely busy
CRM: Customer Relationship Management
Crooks: criminals; thieves
Crowdfunding: the practice of funding a project or business venture by raising small amounts of money from a large number of people, especially via the Internet
Crucial: extremely important
Crunch numbers: calculate carefully; do the math
CTO: Chief Technology Officer
Cubicle: a work area that is partly separated from the rest of a room in an office
Currency: money used in a particular country
Curveballs: tricky questions
Customize/customized/customized: build, fit or alter according to individual needs; make according to requirements
Cut back on: reduce the amount of something
Cutting-edge: extremely modern and advanced
Cut to the chase: say what is really important without delay; get to the point
CV: Curriculum Vitae (résumé)

Day off: a day when you're not required to work
DBA: Doing Business As
Dead-end job: a job in which there is little or no chance of progressing to a higher paid position
Deadline: time by which something must be completed
Decaf: decaffeinated coffee
Demand: the amount of a product that customers want to buy
Demand/demanded/demanded: require a lot of attention, time or resources

Dept.: department
Disruption: an interruption in the usual way that something works; an act of delaying or interrupting the regular flow of something
Dive into: start doing something enthusiastically; start working hard
DOB: Date of Birth
Downside: negative aspect of something; disadvantage
Dress code: a set of rules specifying what you can wear for a particular occasion or place
Drone: an aircraft without a pilot that is operated by remote control
Drop the subject: stop talking about it
Dull: boring; not interesting

Eager beaver: a person who is hardworking and enthusiastic
Early bird: someone who wakes up and starts working very early; someone who gets somewhere or does something earlier than anyone else
Earplug: a device to protect the ears from loud noises
Eavesdrop/eavesdropped/eavesdropped: listen secretly to someone's private conversation
EBITDA: Earning Before Interests, Taxes, Depreciation and Amortization
EC: European Community
e.g.: exempli gratia, for example
E-mail/e-mailed/e-mailed: send an e-mail or e-mails to someone
Embezzlement: theft of funds placed in one's trust
Empower/empowered/empowered: equip with an ability; enable
End user: the final user or consumer of a product
Enlightening: clarifying
Enroll/enrolled/enrolled: register formally as a participant of a lecture, show, etc.
Enticed: attracted; interested
Envisage/envisaged/envisaged: imagine or expect something in the future
EPA: Environmental Protection Agency
ERP: Enterprise Resources Planning
ETA: Estimated Time of Arrival
EU: European Union

Expenditure: the act of spending money
Expertise: natural or acquired proficiency in a particular activity; ability; skill
Expo: exposition; public exhibition

Face charges: be officially accused of committing a crime
Facilities: equipment and services provided for a particular purpose
Fair: exhibition; exposition; show
FAQ: Frequently Asked Questions
FDA: Food and Drug Administration
Feasible: viable; capable of being done or achieved.
Features: important aspects of something
Figures: numbers
File a lawsuit against someone: sue someone
Fill in for: substitute
Findings: information that is discovered as a result of investigation
Find out: discover
Fire/fired/fired: dismiss from employment
First-hand: coming directly from the original source
Fit in: be accepted by a group o people
Flash drive: a small device used to store digital data
FOB: Free on Board
Food for thought: something that makes you think seriously
For all I know: as far as I know
Forklifts: small vehicles which have two metal bars fixed to the front used for lifting piles of goods
Freebie: something given or received without charge, usually provided as part of a promotional scheme
Free of charge: without any payment; for free
FYI: For Your Information

Gadget: small electronic device or appliance
Game plan: plan of action; strategy
GDP: Gross Domestic Product

Geek: an expert in a technical field, esp. computers
Get a kick out of: enjoy something greatly
Get along with: have a friendly relationship with
Get down to business: start to work; be serious about something
Get going: leave
Get into the swing of things: become fully involved in an activity and start to understand how it works
Get something off one's chest: tell someone about something that has been annoying you
Getting into the swing of things: starting to understand how something works
Gimmick: a marketing trick used to attract people's attention and interest
GNP: Gross National Product
Go easy on: take it easy on something; not use too much of something
Goggles: protective glasses
Going on: happening
Goods: items for sale; products
Google/googled/googled: search for information on the Web, normally using the Google search engine
Go public: sell shares of a privately owned company to the public
Gotta: have to
Grab a bite: eat something
Graduate school: a school in a university where students who already have a first degree can study for a master's degree or a doctorate
Grand opening: official opening of a new business
Grasp: understanding of something
Gung-ho: very enthusiastic or excited about something

Hacker: a computer programmer who uses his skills to gain illegal access to a computer network in order to steal, change or destroy information
Handle/handled/handled: deal with
Handout: a piece of paper with information that is given to people attending a speech, lecture, etc
Hands-on: involving active participation; relating to practical experience

Hardworking: tending to work seriously and with commitment; habitually working hard; diligent
Haste makes waste: hurrying can cause people to make mistakes
Have their hands full: they are very busy
Head honcho: the most important person in an organization; the top boss
Heading towards: moving toward
Headquarters: main corporate office
Hear through the grapevine: hear news that has been passed from one person to another
Hectic: marked by intense activity; very busy
Highlights: the most significant or interesting parts of something
Hire/hired/hired: employ
Hit a snag: run into an expected problem or difficulty
Hit the shelves: arrive in the stores; be available for sale
Holding company: a company that controls other companies through stock ownership
HQ: Headquarters
HR: Human Resources
Huge: enormous; very big

I

Idle time: a period during which a machine or employee is inactive
   IMF: International Monetary Fund
Inc: Incorporated
Income: a company's profit in a particular period of time; payment received for goods or services or from other sources
Info: Information
Ingenious: very clever; innovative
Inside information: secret information about an organization
Instill/instilled/instilled: introduce an idea gradually into someone's mind
Intern: a student or recent graduate who works in a job in order to gain experience
Internship: a job that a college student does for a short time in order to gain practical experience of a type of work
Intranet: a private computer network that can be accessed only by the employees of a company
IOU: I Owe You

IP: Internet Protocol
IPO: Initial Public Offering
IRS: Internal Revenue Service
ISO: International Standardization Organization
ISP: Internet Service Provider
Issue: a problem or question
IT: Information Technology

Jet lag: the feeling of tiredness and confusion that people experience when crossing time zones during long flights
JIT: Just In Time
Jump ship: leave a post or position, job or activity suddenly, before it is finished

K: thousand
KBI: Key Business Indicators
Keep me posted: keep me informed
Keep you posted: keep you informed
Key: important
Keynote speaker: someone who gives the main talk at a conference
Keynote speech: the main speech at an event.
Kind: generous; pleasant; nice
Kink: small problem

Laid-back: calm and relaxed; easy-going; not worried about things that need to be done
Land/landed/landed: get something desirable such as a job or an opportunity
LASER: Light Amplification by Stimulated Emission of Radiation
Launch: an event to introduce a new product
Launder/laundered/laundered: convert illegally obtained funds into legal ones

Lawsuit: a legal proceeding in a court of law involving a claim, complaint, etc.
Lb: pound
LCD: Liquid Crystal Display
Lecture: an instructive talk given to a group of people
Leisure: free time from work or duties
Let's take one step at a time: let's do things gradually, without rushing
Likely: probable
Loan shark: someone who lends money at excessive rates of interest
Logistics: the planning and management of the details of an operation
Logo: a symbol used by a company; logotype
Looking up: getting better; improving
Lubricate/lubricated/lubricated: apply an oily or greasy substance to a machine in order to reduce friction

M&A: mergers and acquisitions
Make a killing: earn a lot of money quickly
Make of: think of
Marketplace: the world of business and commerce
Market share: the percentage of sales of a particular product or products held by a company
Massive: huge; very large in amount or degree
Mastermind/masterminded/masterminded: plan and organize a complex operation, often a crime
Maternity leave: a period of time a woman is legally allowed to be away from work in the weeks before and after she has a baby
Matter: problem; trouble
Max: maximum
MBA: Master of Business Administration
Meet a deadline: finish something in time
Memo: memorandum
Merge/merged/merged: join or combine into a single organization; become one
Merger: the combination of two or more companies to form a bigger one; when two or more companies get together to form a bigger one
Micromanage/micromanaged/micromanaged: manage or control a business or project with excessive attention to details

GLOSSARY 159

Mindset: way of thinking; mentality
Mingle/mingled/mingled: socialize; participate actively in a social group
Morale: the amount of confidence and enthusiasm felt by a person or group of people
Moving to the next level: improving or developing even more
Multitasker: a person who can do several things at the same time

N/A: Not Applicable
Narrow-minded: not willing to accept new ideas, opinions or behavior that are different from your own
NASDAQ: National Association of Securities Dealers Automated Quotation
Networking: the practice of meeting other people involved in the same kind of work to exchange information
NGO: Non-governmental Organization
NLP: Neurolinguistic Programming
no.: number
Nope: no
No rush: no hurry
NPO: Non-Profit Organization; Not for Profit Organization
NYSE: New York Stock Exchange

Office supplies: supplies used in offices, such as paper clips, staples and A4 paper
On a daily basis: every day
On behalf of: speaking for; as a representative of
On duty: doing one's job; at work
On leave: absent with permission from work or duty
On top of things: in control of what is happening
OPEC: Organization of the Petroleum Exporting Countries
Opening: an available job or position
Organization chart: a diagram showing the management structure of a company
Other than that: besides that

Outgoing: friendly and sociable; extroverted
Outlet: market for goods; a store where a particular product is sold
Out of the question: impossible
Output: the amount of something produced; goods or services produced by a company
Outsource/outsourced/outsourced: use a third-party service provider to execute a business function; obtain services from an outside supplier
Outstanding: very good; excellent
Overlook/overlooked/overlooked: fail to see or consider; ignore
Overseas: abroad
Overtime: extra hours that someone works in addition to their usual job hours
Overwhelmed: struck by an intense emotional reaction
Overwhelming: very great or strong

p. a.: per annum, per year
Pain in the neck: something that is annoying or irritating
Pal: close friend; buddy
Pan out/panned out/panned out: develop in a particular way; have a specified result; turn out well
Paradigm: a model of something; a typical example or pattern of something
Paradigm shift: the time when the usual way of doing something changes completely; a radical change in ideas or beliefs
Pass away: die
Payroll: a list of employees and their salaries; the total amount of money paid to employees
pd.: paid
Peer: someone who belongs to the same professional group as another person
Pending issue: something that still needs to be dealt with
Perks: benefits beyond regular pay
Phase out: gradually stop manufacturing a product, etc.
PIN: Personal Identification Number
Plain: honest; open

Plaintiff: complaining party in a lawsuit
Plan ahead: make preparations or arrangements for the future
Plant: factory
Play a key role: have a big influence on; be very important
Played an important role: had a big influence; was very important
Player: influential person, company or organization, esp. in business or politics
Play hardball: work or act aggressively, competitively or ruthlessly
Plenty: a large amount of something
Pls: please
Plummet/plummeted/plummeted: fall quickly; decrease rapidly in value or amount
P.M.: Post Meridiem, after noon
PO: Post Office
Policy: a plan of action intended to guide decisions; procedure
Pop up: appear suddenly or unexpectedly
P.R.: Public Relations
Press conference: an interview in which a politician or famous person gives information to television reporters and answers questions.
Pricy: expensive
Prime time: the hours when television audiences are largest
Printout: a document printed from a printer
Product line: a group of products marketed by a company
Prospect: potential customer
Prospects: the possibility of future success
P.S.: Postscript
p.t.o.: please turn over
Pull someone's leg: tell someone something that's not true as a joke
Purchase/purchased/purchased: buy
Put out fires: deal with urgent problems at work
Put together: create something; organize something using different pieces or parts
Put up with: tolerate
p.w.: per week

QC: Quality Control

Qty: quantity
Quarter: a period of three months

Rapport: harmonious relationship
Raw material: basic material used in manufacture
R&D: Reseach and Development
Reap the rewards: enjoy the results of something
Recharge one's batteries: rest for a period of time in order to feel energetic again
Recruit: a new member in a company or an organization, especially someone who has recently been hired
Red tape: too much paperwork that slows down business; bureaucracy
Redundant: unnecessary; not needed
Release/released/released: make a product, movie, CD, etc. available for people to buy
Reschedule/rescheduled/rescheduled: assign a new date for something to happen
Resign/resigned/resigned: give up a job or position formally
Resilient: able to recover from difficulty; recovering quickly from adversity
Résumé: summary of one's academic qualifications and work experience
Retail: the selling of goods to consumers; usually in small quantities and not for resale
ROI: Return On Investment
Roll up one's sleeves: get ready to start work
Rough: difficult; tough
RSI: Repetitive Strain Injury
RSVP: Répondez S'il Vous Plaît, please reply
Run a business: manage a business; be in charge of a company
Run into: meet or find someone by chance
Run low on: run out of; be almost spent or finished
Running: managing; taking care of
Rush hour: the time of day when traffic is heavy because many people are going to or coming from work
Rush into things: do or say something before it should be done or said

Sales rep: sales representative
Sample: piece or item, such as of a product, that shows the quality of the whole
Scam: a fraudulent business scheme, a dishonest plan for making money
Sci-fi: science fiction
Scumbag: a low, worthless person
Set up a meeting: schedule a meeting
Set up shot: start a business; create a place to do business
Shady: dishonest or illegal
Shareholder: someone who owns stocks in a corporation
Shift: a period of work time
Ship/shipped/shipped: send products to customers by air or land
Short-staffed: without enough workers
Showcase/showcased/showcased: show the best qualities of something
Show up: come; appear; arrive
Shut down: stop operating, esp. a factory
Silicon Valley: a region in California well-known for its concentration of high-tech industries
Slot machine: a gambling machine operated by inserting coins into a slot
Small talk: light, informal conversation about things that are not important
Smoothly: with no problems or difficulties
Snag: unexpected difficulty
Snazzy: fashionable; modern and stylish
Social media: websites that enable people to share content and engage in social networking
So far: until now
So far so good: everything is OK up to this point
Someday: at some future time
Spare part: a replacement component for a machine
Speech: a talk given to an audience
Speed up: make something move or happen faster
Sponsor: a company that pays all or part of the cost of an event usually in exchange for advertising its products.
Sponsor/sponsored/sponsored: pay for an event (a sporting or artistic event or a television or radio program) in return for advertising

Spreadsheet: a computer program for financial calculations
Staff: a group of people who work for a company
Stand a fair chance: have a good chance
Start from scratch: start a project from the very beginning; start from nothing
Start-up: a new business that has just been started
State-of-the-art: very modern; at the highest level of development
Stationery: pens, pencils, paper, envelopes, etc.; office materials
Stationery store: a store that sells pens, pencils, paper, envelopes, etc.
Stats: statistics
Streamline/streamlined/streamlined: simplify a process in order to increase its efficiency
Suck you dry: drain all your money
Sue/sued/sued: take legal action against a person or organization; file a lawsuit against
Supportive: giving support or assistance; helpful and sympathetic
Swamped (with work): overburdened with work
Swindle/swindled/swindled: obtain money dishonestly from a person or a company
SWOT: Strengths, Weaknesses, Opportunities and Threats
Sympathy: ability to understand or share the feelings or interests of another; compassion

T

Tablet: a type of lightweight portable computer
Tag: a small piece of paper attached to something to give information about it, such as price, etc.
Tailor-made: made to specific requirements
Take a rain check: postpone until a later time
Take a toll on: show wear and tear on someone or something; damage
Take one step at a time: do things gradually, without rushing
Take place: happen; occur
Take time off: have free time from work; take a break or vacation
Talk: an informal lecture
Talk shop: talk about work or business during free time

Tan: suntan; the dark color of someone's skin after intensive exposure to the sun
Tax haven: a country, state or independent region where taxes are low
Taxpayer: someone who pays taxes
Team player: someone who works well with others
Teamwork: cooperative effort done by a team in order to achieve a common goal
The clock is ticking: time is going by quickly
The pros and cons: the good and bad aspects of a situation; the advantages and disadvantages
Think big: set high goals; have big plans and ideas
Think it over: consider something carefully
Think out of the box: think freely, in an innovative way, using new ideas instead of traditional ones
Thought-provoking: that stimulates interest and thought; that makes you think of new ideas
Time-consuming: that takes a long time to do
Timeline: a plan that shows when something should happen and how long it will take
Tip: useful piece of information or advice
Tip of the iceberg: small part of a problem that is really much larger
TM: Trademark
Touch base with: get in touch with; maintain contact
Tough it out: go on with something in spite of difficulties; stand a situation
TQM: Total Quality Management
Trade fair: trade show; a large event at which companies show their products to prospective customers
Trademark: a registered name, symbol or design identifying a particular company
Trade show: trade fair; a large event at which companies show their products to prospective customers
Trend: general direction in which something tends to move; prevailing tendency
Trial: hearing and judgment of a matter in a court of law
Tricks of the trade: special knowledge associated with a profession
Try/tried/tried: judge a person or case in a court of law
Turnover: the rate at which employees leave a company and are replaced

TV spots: a short section between TV programs used for advertising
Twenty-four seven: twenty-four hours per day, seven days per week; all the time

Underestimate/underestimated/underestimated: consider someone or something to be less important, intelligent, smaller or capable than they really are
Unrivaled: incomparable; having no rival; better than any other of the same type
Unveil/unveiled/unveiled: make something secret known or public; reveal; disclose
Upcoming: happening soon; approaching
Up and running: actively working; functioning
Up in the air: uncertain; not yet decided
Ups and downs: highs and lows; good and bad times
Upside: a positive or advantageous aspect

VAT: Value Added Tax
Venue: place where a public event or meeting happens
VIP: Very Important Person
VoIP: Voice-over Internet Protocol
VP: Vice President

Warehouse: a place for storage of goods
We all have our hands full: we are all busy
What have you been up to?: what have you been doing?
What's up?: what's going on?; what's the matter?
What's your take?: what's your opinion?
Whine/whined/whined: complain
Wholesale: the selling of goods in large quantities to stores and businesses for resale to consumers.
Wi-Fi: Wireless Fidelity

GLOSSARY 167

Willing: inclined or disposed
Winner: something very popular or successful
Winning streak: a series of wins
Win-win situation: a situation where both or all parties benefit from a deal
Wisely: prudently; showing good sense or good judgment
Witness: someone who sees an event, such as a crime, accident, etc. and reports what happened; testimony
Wk.: week
w/o: without
Workaholic: someone with a compulsive need to work
Workforce: the workers employed by a company
Workload: the amount of work that a person has to do
Workplace: the places where people work
Workstation: a desk with a computer in an office for someone to work at
Worst-case scenario: the worst thing that could possibly happen
Wrap it up: finish it
Wrapping up: finishing
Wrongdoing: illegal or dishonest behavior
WTO: World Trade Organization
www: world wide web

Yep: yes
You can say that again: you are right; that's true (to agree with a statement)
You got the picture: you understood
You have a point: you are right; I agree with you
You nailed it: you got it right!; that's exactly it
Yuppie: Young Urban Professional

Este livro foi composto nas fontes Expo Sans e Expo Serif
e impresso em abril de 2018 pela Orgrafic Gráfica e Editora Ltda.,
sobre papel offset 75g/m².